THE HOLOCAUST

Selected Documents in Eighteen Volumes

John Mendelsohn
EDITOR

Donald S. Detwiler
ADVISORY EDITOR

A GARLAND SERIES

CONTENTS OF THE SERIES

THE HOLOCAUST

7. Jewish Emigration
The S.S. *St. Louis* Affair
and Other Cases

Introduction by
John Mendelsohn

GARLAND PUBLISHING, INC.
NEW YORK · LONDON
1982

These documents have been reproduced from copies in
the National Archives. Dr. Mendelsohn's work was carried out entirely on his own time and without endorsement or official participation by the National Archives as
an agency.

Library of Congress Cataloging in Publication Data
Main entry under title:

Jewish emigration—the SS St. Louis affair and other cases.

(The Holocaust ; 7)
1. Jews—Germany—Migrations—Sources.
2. Germany—Emigration and immigration—Sources.
3. Cuba—Emigration and immigration—Sources.
4. St. Louis (Ship)   I. Series.
D810.J4H655   vol. 7   940.53'15'03924s   81-80315
[DS135.G33]   [940.53'15'03924]   AACR2
ISBN 0-8240-4881-4

Design by Jonathan Billing

The volumes in this series have been printed on acid-free,
250-year-life paper.

Printed in the United States of America

ACKNOWLEDGMENTS

I owe a debt of gratitude to many people who aided me during various stages of preparing these eighteen volumes. Of these I would like to mention by name a few without whose generous efforts this publication would have been impossible. I would like to thank Donald B. Schewe of the Franklin D. Roosevelt Library in Hyde Park, New York, for his speedy and effective help. Sally Marcks and Richard Gould of the Diplomatic Branch of the National Archives in Washington, D.C., extended help beyond their normal archival duties, as did Timothy Mulligan and George Wagner from the Modern Military Branch. Edward J. McCarter in the Still Picture Branch helped a great deal. I would also like to thank my wife, Tish, for letting me spend my evenings during the past few years with these volumes rather than with her and our children, Michael and Lisa.

J. M.

INTRODUCTION

During the six months preceding the outbreak of World War II in September 1939 emigration increased dramatically. This was largely due to increased Nazi pressure, foresight on the part of many Jews, and greater possibilities for emigration brought about by the work of the Intergovernmental Committee on Refugees and private organizations. One of the most stirring events in the drama of Jewish emigration from Germany during this period was the SS *St. Louis* affair. Because of a concentrated Nazi effort to force Jews to emigrate, ever larger numbers of Jews began to leave Germany in the spring of 1939, when it seemed easier for them to obtain visas or landing permits. In fact, the Cuban director of emigration, Colonel Manuel Benitez, had sold many landing permits wholesale to the Hamburg-Amerika Linie. The passenger ship line resold these permits to individual Jews, often for as much as $160 apiece. A shift in Cuban emigration policies caused by an internal power struggle invalidated these permits, but the line failed to inform the passengers of the cancellation. Thus when some nine hundred Jewish passengers arrived at Havana, the port authorities did not permit them to disembark.

Extensive negotiations led to nothing, and the SS *St. Louis* was forced to turn around. To return to Nazi Germany was out of the question for the desperate passengers. Fortunately, however, after hours of intense drama the Netherlands, Belgium, France, and Great Britain agreed to grant asylum to the emigrants. But their plight did not end there. The safe haven proved to be only a way station, as many who landed in the Netherlands, Belgium, and France found themselves in the Auschwitz extermination factory after Hitler's blitz overran those countries.

Emigration, almost brought to a stop by the German invasion of the Soviet Union, nonetheless continued to provide a slight avenue of escape for some Jews. The entrance of the United States into the war further narrowed this channel, and the Nazi government exerted efforts to prevent any further emigration of Jews after this time. Negotiations with the German foreign office to permit five thousand Jewish children to emigrate to Palestine during this phase of the war failed because the Nazis had no intention of letting the children go, but just played along for propaganda purposes. The stated reason for their final refusal was that they could not have "the noble Arab people be settled with such inferior stock."

Some of the nine hundred Jewish refugees from Germany on board the SS *St. Louis* in Havana harbor, looking for friends and relatives who have drawn alongside in launches. June 3, 1939.

National Archives and Records Service 306-NT-648-E-5

The documents reproduced in this volume were selected from five document collections: the Nuernberg Trials prosecution document series, the central decimal file of the Department of State, the records of the German foreign ministry, those of the Reich leader of the SS and the chief of the German police, and the Ira Hirschmann papers in the Franklin Delano Roosevelt Library. These records document the SS *St. Louis* affair and the fate of Jewish emigrants on other vessels. Some deal with reports of Jews emigrating from Poland, Yugoslavia, and Germany and with restrictions placed on emigration by the Nazis in view of the coming "Final Solution." Other documents pertain to the futile attempts to gain permission for five thousand Jewish children to emigrate from Nazi-held territory in 1943.

John Mendelsohn

SOURCE ABBREVIATIONS
AND DESCRIPTIONS

Nuernberg Document

Records from five of the twenty-five Nuernberg Trials prosecution document series: the NG (Nuernberg Government) series, the NI (Nuernberg Industrialist) series, the NO (Nuernberg Organizations) series, the NOKW (Nuernberg Armed Forces High Command) series, and the PS (Paris-Storey) series. Also included are such Nuernberg Trials prosecution records as interviews, interrogations, and affidavits, excerpts from the transcripts of the proceedings, briefs, judgments, and sentences. These records were used by the prosecution staff of the International Military Tribunal at Nuernberg or the twelve United States military tribunals there, and they are part of National Archives Record Group 238, National Archives Collection of World War II War Crimes Records.

OSS

Reports by the Office of Strategic Services in National Archives Record Group 226.

SEA

Staff Evidence Analysis: a description of documents used by the Nuernberg prosecution staff. Although the SEA's tended to describe only the evidentiary parts of the documents in the summaries, they describe the document title, date, and sources quite accurately.

State CDF

Central Decimal File: records of the Department of State in National Archives Record Group 59, General Records of the Department of State.

T 120

Microfilm Publication T 120: records of the German foreign office received from the Department of State in Record Group 242, National Archives Collection of Foreign Records Seized, 1941–. The following citation system is used for National Archives

Microfilm Publications: The Microfilm Publication number followed by a slash, the roll number followed by a slash, and the frame number(s). For example, Document 1 in Volume I: T 120/4638/K325518—K325538.

T 175

Microfilm Publication T 175: records of the Reich leader of the SS and of the chief of the German police in Record Group 242.

U.S. Army and U.S. Air Force

Records relating to the attempts to cause the U.S. Army Air Force to bomb the extermination facilities at Auschwitz and the railroad center at Kaschau leading to Auschwitz, which are part of a variety of records groups and collections in the National Archives. Included are records of the United States Strategic Bombing Survey (Record Group 243), records of the War Refugee Board (Record Group 220), records of the Joint Chiefs of Staff, and other Army record collections.

War Refugee Board

Records of the War Refugee Board, located at the Franklin D. Roosevelt Library in Hyde Park, New York. They are part of National Archives Record Group 220, Records of Temporary Committees, Commissions and Boards. Included in this category are the papers of Myron C. Taylor and Ira Hirschmann.

CONTENTS

Notes

1. *Documents 5 and 6.* The telegrams are from Joseph P. Kennedy, the American ambassador in London.

2. *Documents 8 and 9.* The SS *St. Louis* was not the only vessel that encountered difficulties in safely landing its desperate passengers. The Woermann Linie steamer *Wangoni* and the English steamer *Orduna* had similar problems.

3. *Document 14.* Franz Rademacher was an official in department Inland II of the German foreign ministry, which provided liaison with the Reich leader of the SS, Heinrich Himmler, and subordinate SS agencies.

4. *Document 16.* Horst Wagner was the chief of department Inland II.

V O L U N T A R Y

S T R I C T L Y   C O N F I D E N T I A L

No. 311

EUROPEAN REFUGEES IN CUBA

From:

Harold S. Tewell
American Consul

American Consulate General, Habana, Cuba.	Date of Completion:	March 17, 1939
	Date of Mailing:	March 18, 1939

File No. 811.11/855

HST/jml

Distribution:
  Original and four copies to the Department;
  One copy to the Embassy.

There are in Cuba at this time approximately 2,500 Jewish refugees from Europe, chiefly Germany and Poland. For the most part they are congregated in the city of Habana, where about 300 are dependent upon the relief provided by the Joint Relief Committee of the National Coordinating Committee, i. e., relief provided by residents of the United States. This relief consists of an allowance of $7 a week for each destitute refugee. In addition the Committee administers private funds, provided by residents of the United States, for destitute relatives or friends in Cuba. In other words, at least $10,000 monthly at present is being provided by residents of the United States for the support of European refugees in Cuba.

2

Approximately half of the Jewish refugees in Cuba are registered as applicants for visas to enter the United States for permanent residence. Not included in this category are the 300 persons on relief. It is the writer's information that the latter consist largely of aliens that undoubtedly wish to enter the United States but who are without relatives or friends able and willing to guarantee that they will not become public charges. It is stated, however, that in this number also are aliens whose relatives and friends in the United States do not wish them to enter the latter country but who prefer to contribute to their maintenance in Cuba through relief organizations, or by providing funds directly, as mentioned above. It is understood that this attitude of Jewish residents of the United States is based upon the belief that the influx of a considerable number of dependent members of their race would incite in the United States

widespread

widespread organized opposition to the further entry of all Jews, and possible unfavorable reaction upon members of that race now residing in the United States.

The remaining members of the refugee colony--the 1,000 or more who have not indicated any intention of entering the United States--have come to Cuba as one of the few countries in the world open to them, either as permanent residents or to reside here at least until they determine what more definite plans, if any, can be made as to a future home. For the reasons explained hereafter it may be concluded that a large part of these also are potential applicants for admission to the United States. Accordingly it may be estimated that of the present refugee colony, from 1,800 to 2,000 will endeavor, sooner or later, to obtain immigration visas to enter the United States.

Except the 300 destitute refugees on organized relief and those who receive assistance directly from relatives in the United States, these aliens are possessed of certain financial resources--usually a few hundred dollars, although a few may be said to have quite ample means, salvaged remains of substantial wealth accumulated in their native lands. The latter are applicants for admission to the United States, with few exceptions, for they have the financial means to wait the long period (from one to three years) before quota numbers now may be expected to become available for their use. Of course it is probable that a number of aliens having limited financial resources may find it necessary to establish

themselves

3

themselves in business at least temporarily in Cuba,
especially those that must rely solely upon their own
resources to establish admissibility to the United States
when quota numbers may become available for their use.
A few may even decide to remain here in business, and
abandon their intention to enter the United States.

The present Cuban colony of refugees for the most
part has developed within the past seven months, and it
is anticipated that, barring unforeseen circumstances, it
will henceforth greatly increase. It is estimated that
the influx of European refugees into Cuba is now taking
place at the rate of 500 monthly, and included in recent
arrivals were a few Jews from Italy. The extent to which
this influx will continue depends in a large measure upon
the continuance of the present Cuban immigration procedure that permits European refugees to enter this country,
as discussed later in this report.

Colonization Plans

Recognizing that most refugees have not the financial
resources or assistance of relatives to sustain them in
idleness for an indefinite and long period of years, and
in view of the existing procedure for their admission to
Cuba, there recently has been made an investigation and
tentative plan, for presentation to American Jewish relief agencies, to promote the emigration of thousands of
European refugees to this country for permanent residence.
It is understood from those interested that of all countries in the western hemisphere (except the United States)
Cuba offers, apparently, the most opportunities and

advantageous

advantageous facilities for refugees.

At least one such plan, of which the details have been canvassed, involves the admission to Cuba of not less than 25,000 European refugees, Jewish and gentile, who would be established in a specially developed community on the Isle of Pines. While the community in question would be largely agricultural--fruit and vegetable growing, poultry farming, and dairying--certain other industries to supply the wants of the community also would be established, and if possible, manufacturing industries to supply for domestic consumption goods not now made in Cuba, as well as other factories to manufacture articles chiefly for export.

Inquiry by those investigating this plan, is stated to have disclosed that there are available on the Isle of Pines in one block, thousands of acres of unimproved agricultural land at a price approximating $3.00 an acre. While extensive tracts of land in the northern portion of the Isle of Pines formerly cultivated (largely citrus fruit groves) by and at present held by American citizens, are understood to be available at low prices ($5.00 to $10.00 an acre), the area now deemed most suitable for a refugee colony is understood to lie on the very sparsely populated south coast of the Isle. This is believed to be chiefly swamp land at present covered by a dense growth of underbrush and considerable merchantable timber, but provided with a likely harbor site and natural sandy beaches. In view of the character of the land made productive by the Jewish population of Palestine, those who have investigated the southern coast of the Isle of Pines

5

declare

declare that it presents no insuperable difficulties as
to drainage and other improvements necessary to make it
productive. The Cuban Government is understood to be
constructing (with the aid of prisoners from the peniten-
tiary) a highway from the town of Santa Fé to the south
coast of the Isle, for which work the sum of $10,000 has
been allotted. The highway in question traverses thinly
settled lands owned by American citizens and larger areas
occupied at present by Cuban cattlemen, and its purpose
or value is not apparent unless it forms part of a colonization plan (1).

Cuban interests with which negotiations have been
conducted by those interested in developing a refugee
colony, are understood to have in hand the acquiring of
sufficient land for the purpose as well as arranging, by
means of a decree, for the admission to Cuba of a stated
number of European refugees without the requirement of
bonds or the payment of any fees to the Cuban Government.
This arrangement, it is stated, will be made with the
understanding that such refugees may not seek employment
in Cuba outside the proposed colony, and that they will
reside only in such colony, although they may be permitted
to visit temporarily or pass through other Cuban territory
on business or for pleasure.

It is understood to be the idea of those who have
investigated this project, for presentation to American
Jewish relief organizations, that the land on the Isle of

Pines

- -
(1) According to rumor this highway, however, concerns
military interest on the part of the United States in
certain developments on the Isle of Pines.

Pines that it may be deemed necessary to acquire for the
establishment of a refugee colony (for Jews as well as
gentiles), will be purchased by an American corporation
formed for that purpose and that funds of the corporation
will be obtained by the sale of bonds, chiefly among the
Jewish population of the United States. The land so acquired would be divided into tracts suitable for various
agricultural pursuits and would be sold to refugees on
long terms, with the provision that should the purchaser
leave the colony his land must be resold only to the
Corporation.

Another colonization plan, which is understood to
involve no assistance from American Jewish relief agencies,
is under consideration by an applicant for a visa to enter
the United States--a Jewish native of Czecho-Slovakia who
is stated to have substantial financial resources. This
proposal involves also the purchase of a tract of some
65,000 acres of land on the southeastern coast of the Isle
of Pines at a stated cost of $30,000. This property, under
one ownership, is stated to carry a mortgage of $22,000,
which would be assumed by the purchaser.

To colonise this tract it is proposed to bring to
Cuba several hundred Jewish citizens of Czecho-Slovakia,
each having at least $1,500 to $2,000 in cash. The colony
would be devoted to agricultural as well as manufacturing
enterprises, among the latter being the manufacture of
earthenware (for which raw materials of a quality much
superior to those in Czecho-Slovakia are said to be available in abundance); the production of mahogany lumber and ﹍

7

manufacture

manufacture of articles of wood; and textile manufacturing, 80 prospective members of the colony being experts in the Czecho-Slovakian textile industry. Tentative arrangements are stated to have been made with Cuban authorities for the entry of these colonists under cash bonds of $500 each, such deposit to be refunded at the expiration of two years if the alien concerned meantime has not become a public charge, or upon his departure from Cuba within that period, as provided in Decree No. 55 of January 13, 1939 (1).

Regarding the fertility of land in the northern portion of the Isle of Pines there appears to be little doubt, since the settlement of that region many years ago by hundreds of Americans, largely engaged in fruit and vegetable growing, has definitely established its productivity. When the Isle of Pines ceased to be American territory fourteen years ago residents also lost the principal market for their products. The depression that followed shortly after, and other subsequent events have served but to accentuate the fact that there is no profitable market for Isle of Pines fruit and vegetables. Seasonal tariff concessions made in the Reciprocal Trade Agreement of 1934 have had but little remedial effect. Under the circumstances, while a colony of 25,000 in itself would offer an outlet for a certain amount of farm produce, there is little reason to expect that a community of European Jews could find the necessary profitable export market for surplus production when Americans have been unable to so do.

The

- -
(1) See report "New Cuban Law Regarding Admission of
      aliens", January 19, 1939.

The latter, in fact, would welcome the opportunity to dispose of their land holdings on the Isle of Pines to such a foreign colony.

Even less promising, it appears, is the proposal to establish an agricultural settlement on the south coast of the Isle. Residents of long standing report that the region in question, while containing patches of soil, is comprised largely of areas of coral formation of no value whatever from an agricultural standpoint. Once denuded of its timber the coastal region is stated to offer very few resources of economic value.

Because of the equable climate, the presence of certain mineral water springs, sandy beaches, and access to game fishing grounds, it appears that a colony with some capital and initiative might encourage a profitable winter tourist traffic during the winter months. There may be an opportunity to develop other industries on the Isle of Pines, but it does not appear that any agricultural development of importance profitably can be undertaken under existing circumstances.

The Cuban interests endeavoring to interest American Jewish relief organizations in establishing a refugee colony on the Isle of Pines have organized under the name Compañía Colonizadora Industrial, S.A., formed on March 3, 1939, with the following officers: Luis A. Moreno, President; Adalberto Masvidal, Vice President; Celestino Blanch, Treasurer; Rene Benitez, Assistant Treasurer; Dr. del Pino, Secretary, and Dr. Raul F. Mederos, Assistant Secretary. The company is understood to have practically no financial resources, but it is stated to have obtained options on a

                                              substantial

9

substantial acreage of land on the Isle of Pines, chiefly
from the American owners thereof. The officers of the
company are not prominent residents of Habana, but two
or three of them are known to have connections in political circles that may or may not be influential, depending
upon changing circumstances.

The Admission of Refugees to Cuba

For more than a year European refugees have been
coming to Habana to remain temporarily until they can obtain quota immigration visas to enter the United States.
When this traffic assumed some proportions and gave evidence of continuing indefinitely, the Cuban Director General
of Immigration, on June 1, 1938, issued a circular out-
lining the requirements for admission to this country of
various categories of aliens. This circular provided that
aliens, classified as transients, entering this country to
make application for visas to enter the United States, if
not entering from the United States, each must file a bond
of $200 in the event visas to enter the United States
should be refused. Aliens of the immigrant class, however,
were required to post cash bonds of $500, and to obtain
from the Director General of Immigration in advance of
their arrival, permission to land in Cuba. This was handled
through the steamship lines concerned.

On November 17, 1938 the Cuban Government took further
recognizance of the European refugee situation by promul-
gating Decree No. 2507, the preamble of which read as follows:

"The

> "The Republic of Cuba has the right to
> select the quality of immigrants most suited
> to the development of the population, its
> industries and commerce, classifying each im-
> migrant as useful or not useful to our nation-
> ality."

This measure introduced the passport visa for the first
time as a requirement for admission to Cuba "temporarily
or permanently", although it exempted (paragraph 3) from
such requirement tourists and transit passengers. This
was followed on January 15, 1939 with Decree No. 55, which
exempted (Article 4-a) from the $500 cash bond require-
ment tourists, transients, and in transit passengers as
well as other classes of non-immigrants, and modified
the provision of Decree No. 2507 with regard to the passport visa requirement, to read as follows:

> "Diplomatic and consular officers of the
> Republic will report all cases of foreigners
> who, being required to make a deposit in com-
> pliance with the immigration regulations, in-
> tend to go to Cuba; they will indicate the
> habitual profession or occupation of such for-
> eigners and, in those cases, they will subject
> the visa procedure to authorization from the
> Department of State, to be given after hearing
> the opinions of the Departments of the Treasury
> and of Labor."

Accordingly, at present aliens of the immigrant class require a passport visa and a $500 cash bond to enter Cuba,
while non-immigrant aliens, except tourists and transit
passengers, are required to have passport visas, but no
bonds. Tourists and transit passengers require neither
visas nor bonds.

It is understood that many refugees and other aliens
entering Cuba to make application for visas for admission
to the United States now are classified as tourists, who,

under

under Decree No. 55 are defined as "those persons travel-
ing for pleasure and who do not engage in any labor during their sojourn in the national territory". To obtain
this classification, involving no visa or bond, it is
understood that payment of an unofficial fee of from $100
to $150 is necessary. In such cases a letter, as follows,
is issued by the Director General of Immigration to the
alien concerned:

> "In view of what is stated by you in the
> sworn declaration presented at this office,
> and in accordance with the provisions of para-
> graph (a) of Article 4 of Presidential Decree
> No. 55, dated January 13, 1939 and paragraph
> third of Decree No. 2507 of November 17, 1938,
> this Bureau has authorized the entrance and
> stay in Cuba, for such time as it may be neces-
> sary to obtain your visa to enter the United
> States of America or any other country, of Mr.
> ...., native of Berlin, Germany; pro-
> vided that he suffers from no illness or phys-
> ical defect, that he has the necessary passport
> and that he does not come to devote himself to
> work of any kind."

This status is arranged and the letter written before the
alien leaves the European port of embarcation, since
transportation lines do not care to undertake to carry
passengers to Cuba that might be refused admission and
also find it impossible to return to their own countries.
It may be noted that the refugees who now are being classified as tourists under the above circumstances cannot
be expected, under present conditions, to receive visas
to enter the United States in less than three years.

Other refugees are understood to arrive in Cuba with
the passport visas with the intention of being classified
as transients, who are defined in Decree No. 55 as "Persons arriving in Cuba for the purpose of continuing
their journey to a foreign port, or returning to the port

of

of departure, provided they do not remain in the national
territory during a period in excess of thirty days and
provided they are in possession of passage necessary for
continuing their journey to the port of destination".
While transients are exempt from the $500 cash bond re-
quirement, upon reaching Cuba many refugees find that
thirty days will not suffice for their purposes and they
also obtain tourist classification upon the payment of
the unofficial fee.

Other refugees, uncertain as to their future plans
but in possession of sufficient funds, have obtained passport visas and filed $500 bonds before they obtained
tickets for Cuba. Upon their arrival they learned that
during the indefinite period that must elapse before bond
arrangements finally are completed it was necessary that
they remain in the immigration detention camp in Habana
at their own expense. By paying the customary unofficial
fee, however, it has been found that immediate admission
under a non-immigrant classification can be arranged.

According to authentic information, from July 1, 1938
to January 16, 1939 (when Decree No. 55 became applicable)
a total of $544,467 had been deposited in the Cuban Treasury
in immigrants' cash bonds; and according to Habana newspapers (1) from the latter date to February 25, 1939, the
sum of $222,563 had been deposited in the Postal Savings
Bank to cover the bonds of 440 Jewish refugees, all of
whom had not yet arrived. The above sums accordingly
represent the bonds of 1,416 aliens deposited in a period
of eight months.

It

- -
(1) EL MUNDO of March 7, 1939.

It will be noted that Decree No. 2507 originally provided that passport visas might be granted to aliens by Cuban consular and diplomatic officers in accordance with instructions of the Department of State, whereas this was subsequently modified by Decree No. 55 to provide that the Department of State may authorize such visas only after consulting the Departments of the Treasury and Labor. In that connection it has been learned that the Secretary of Labor invariably opposes the granting of visas and has prepared a mimeographed form letter addressed to the Director General of Immigration, for use in such cases, which reads as follows:

> "With regard to your letter of _____ I
> have to inform you that according to our
> records it does not appear that any company in
> Cuba has arranged for the protection of any
> exceptions that the laws permit, for the employ-
> ment in this country, nor has it been estab-
> lished that he possesses property

> (Name of alien)

> "Inasmuch as a large number of Cubans
> are available in our labor market, making it
> very difficult the possibility of employing
> aliens, as a result of which their employ-
> ment moreover is prohibited by Article III
> of Decree No. 2583 of 1933, this Department
> is of the opinion that it should be considered
> that he will become a public charge."

It appears that in some cases the Department of State has declined to authorize the issuance of visas where the Secretary of Labor has opposed such action, and friction between the two departments has been indicated in an authoritative unofficial statement that the Secretary of State refuses to be put in the position of requesting anything of the Secretary of Labor in instances where the former may feel that the issuance of a visas is justified in spite of the objections of the

Department

Department of Labor. The Secretary of Labor, on his part,
is stated to complain of the lack of cooperation from
the Immigration Bureau (which is under the Treasury Department), since the latter is disinclined in many instances to act in accordance with the views of the Department of Labor regarding the entry of aliens. This
conflict between departments, especially between the
Department of Labor and the Bureau of Immigration, has
existed for some time, and not long ago the Secretary
of Labor made an effort to have immigration matters placed
under his jurisdiction. While Article XIV of Decree No.
55 of January 13, 1939 provides that "the Secretaries of
State, Treasury, Education and Labor, and the Council of
Administration of the Postal Savings Bank (in which immigrants' cash bonds now are deposited) are charged with
enforcement of the provisions of this Decree, in the
parts concerning each, respectively", it appears that
friction between the departments principally concerned so
far has prevented agreement upon the regulations to be
issued to carry out the provisions of the decree in question.

In the meantime the Director General of Immigration
is handling the admission of European refugees largely according to his own inclination. This policy has certain
implications. In the first place, the various unofficial
fees (1) imposed upon aliens intending to immigrate to

the
- -
(1) $35 for obtaining the release of an immigrant from
the detention station; $160 for obtaining the release
of each $500 bond deposited by immigrants; $100 to $150
for classification as a non-immigrant; and various fees,
depending upon the financial circumstances of the alien,
for an extension of stay in Cuba (for transients).

15

the United States is a severe drain on their resources,
especially in the case of families, and may affect their
eligibility for admission. In one case it is known that
the fees demanded left the alien absolutely penniless and
dependent upon friends. In the second place, it is not
certain that, in the event there should be a change in
administration in the Bureau of Immigration, many aliens
might not be found to be in Cuba illegally according to
the interpretation that might be made of existing regulations. Refugees for the most part are aware of the uncertainty of their standing, especially the large number
that has paid unofficial fees instead of depositing $500
bonds. While the uncertainty arising from this cause of
course is inconsequential as compared with the situation
from which they have escaped in their native lands, it is
a potential cause of restlessness and desire to enter the
United States as quickly as possible. In some cases it may
easily become the incentive to seek the means of entering
the United States illegally.

Illegal Entry of Aliens to United States

Cuba has long been a base from which aliens are smug-
gled into the United States, and while this traffic has
been reduced considerably during the past three or four
years, the present situation has all the factors that
indicate that a resumption of that traffic on a larger
scale may be anticipated in the near future. These factors
may be briefly summarized as follows:

1. The demand for quota visa numbers greatly in
excess of the supply. On the basis of an annual allot-
ment of 16 quota numbers a month, such as the Consulate

General

General has had at its disposal since October, 1938, applicants now registering for visas under the German quota may expect to remain in Cuba at least three years. The situation is much the same with regard to refugees registered under other quotas.

2. The financial resources of many applicants for visas are not sufficient to enable them to live in idleness any great length of time. They cannot obtain work in Cuba because of the labor laws and the opportunities for establishing themselves in business are exceedingly limited, even were they disposed to risk their small capital temporarily in such undertakings.

3. Hundreds of European refugees that have entered· Cuba in recent months with the apparent intention of residing here, eventually will be forced by economic and other conditions to abandon that intention and apply for visas to enter the United States. Should existing circumstances continue to prevail indefinitely it is obvious that they could not expect to receive visas for several years.

4. The cash bond of $500, and the unofficial fees exacted from refugee aliens from time to time by various Cuban authorities, and the probable consequent increase in uncertainty and anxiety as to their status in Cuba, undoubtedly will arouse intense dissatisfaction over a prolonged stay in this country. A continued influx of refugees in large numbers into this country may be expected to intensify public opinion adverse to further following the policy of granting asylum to such aliens, and create an atmosphere unfavorable to those that already

have

17

have been admitted. In this connection it may be noted that the refugees have no government to which they owe allegiance, to which they may appeal for protection in the event of eventual discrimination or violation of the understanding under which they were admitted to Cuba; nor is there in this country any substantial element of Cuban citizens of their own race to exert political influence or pressure to obtain on their behalf a redress of any grievances that may arise.

5. Insofar as refugees admitted to Cuba as immigrants later may prove not to be assets to this country, after they have spent here all or most of their resources, it may be anticipated that no obstacles will be interposed here to prevent their departure for the United States by any means that may be devised. In that connection it should be remembered that there are in operation in Cuba "rings" that make a business of facilitating the illegal entry of aliens into the United States by means of false citizenship and travel documents or smuggling, and that others formerly engaged in that business but await suitable circumstances to resume operations. Although many of these have been apprehended in past years, not one has been prosecuted and punished, although Cuban laws have been violated. (See despatch No. 845 of March 17, 1939, concerning the use of fraudulent documents to enter the United States and despatch No. 817 of March 1, 1939 concerning the visa applications of Sally Feder and Gerardo Frankel.)

The illegal entry into the United States of aliens from Cuba has been accomplished by means of false visas,

Cuban

Cuban citizenship documents, passports, and birth certificates; by smuggling as stowaways on vessels; by smuggling in small boats hired for the purposes; and attempts have been made to smuggle by airplane. Experience indicates that in the past assistance from the Cuban authorities to combat the smuggling of aliens from this country into the United States has been most efficacious only when the Cuban authorities had reason to fear that small vessels carrying aliens clandestinely from this country also might smuggle into Cuba arms and political exiles inimical to the existing Cuban regime. That incentive to cooperation, however, now largely ceases to exist.

Under the circumstances, agencies of the United States Government must rely almost entirely upon their own efforts to prevent alien smuggling from Cuba. Owing to the means employed to land aliens illegally in the United States, and the fact that the first objective of smugglers in most cases is the irregular coast of the Florida peninsula, it is believed that the most effective efforts to combat this traffic are those made at the source. Unquestionably advance information concerning prospective efforts to smuggle aliens or use fraudulent documents is more effective and can be obtained with less expense than efforts to prevent this illegal traffic only by patrolling the coast or highways. Consequently it is believed that plans to combat a prospective increase in the illegal entry of aliens from Cuba should concentrate first upon improved preventive facilities in Habana--more assistance and more funds.

That the Cuban Government may learn from its own experience to what extent fraudulent documents are prepared

and

and used to facilitate the smuggling of European refugees into this country, is indicated in the following newspaper reports published on March 5 and 11, 1939:

> "Colonel Manuel Benitez, Director General of Immigration, yesterday ordered a widespread investigation of charges that an organization here is illegally providing entry permits for refugees from Europe. The accusation was made by Cuba's Consul General in Berlin to the Justice Department. The Consul did not accuse any person or persons specifically."

- - - - - - - - -

> "The Immigration Department yesterday named Otoa de Caturla, high official, to investigate reports that a ring is operating here to illegally permit entry of Jewish refugees from Europe. Aid of the Secret Service has been requested. .... The investigator said he will especially probe cases where immigration bonds have been posted for the refugees before their arrival."

Cuban Opinion Concerning Refugee Immigrants

Because Cuban opinion concerning the entry of thousands of European refugees may ultimately affect future Cuban policy in that regard, and in the meantime may influence many refugees to apply for admission to the United States who now are coming to Cuba to reside, the following public expressions and comment will be of interest.

In an editorial on January 21, 1939 the leading Habana daily newspaper, "Diario de la Marina", observed that Venezuela, with a large, unpopulated territory, possessing great natural resources, and being free of debt, nevertheless is developing an admirable selective immigration and colonization policy with regard to "the Hebrew victims of present racial persecutions in various European countries". Mexico also has rejected such immigrants, with negligible exceptions, "and those mentioned

are

are not the only nations in America which, beginning with the United States, reject Jewish immigration in a manner more or less frank or subject it to limitations in order to prevent an increase in unemployment and all that results from it or from other causes".

"On the other hand we continue receiving freely hundreds of Hebrews, as is shown by the new contingent of 165 who, according to the news, arrived on the 'Iberia', and of these more than 100 appear to have been admitted immediately while some forty only were placed in Camp Tiscornia (immigration detention station), and certainly they also will be admitted because this immigration has financial backing and there is not lacking someone to post for them a bond of $500, returnable if the immigrant leaves the country within two years, or it is concerted into an entrance tax if he remains longer than that period. ....

"But does this mean that the Secretary of Labor has considered necessary and useful the influx of this new contingent of Israelites, or does it mean that the decree in question (No. 55) has not yet been applied¿ If it is the first, for obvious reasons that organization should make public the reasons upon which have been based the granting of admission; if the second, there is inexcusable delay in fulfilling the requirements for making effective a regulation of such importance to this country. Whatever may be the determining reason for which the immigrants in question have been admitted, public opinion has the right to know it and it is in the interest of the responsible authorities to make it perfectly clear.

"Certainly it appears very difficult, not to say impossible, to show the necessity and use of permitting the entry of immigrants who have the status of manual laborers, either by the hundreds or in tens, regardless of their origin, although they may belong to a very superior race. Because if by a hard and very cruel nationalization of labor law there were compelled to leave the country thousands and thousands of Spaniards, many of whom had resided here for many years and had here brought up families and become married to Cubans, and if moreover Antilleans (1) are being repatriated

en

----

(1) Thousands of Haitians have been repatriated by the Cuban Government in the past two years and a newspaper report published on March 16 states that the Secretary of Labor has announced that an additional 25,000 will be repatriated this year at the close of the cane grinding season.

21

en masse as a means of alleviating the unemployment crisis, it is evident that instead of a shortage of labor there still is a surplus in the cities and in the country.

"But if the matter concerns persons that come to develop their activities in trade and industry, it happens that there exists a plethora of commercial establishments, and there is being made an effort to find the method and manner of limiting the number of these. For that purpose it has been thought to regulate their opening, by means of restrictive licenses, and with regard to factories, there is no right to undertake the establishment of others that require for their existence tariff protection at the expense of the well-to-do consumer and the privation of a majority of the population. Of that class there is enough and it does not seem probable that they can be increased without classifying them as parasites. On the other hand, to provide facilities for them would be not only to complicate still more our semi-colonial economy, but to create foolishly new impediments to obtaining possible advantages in trade with the United States, only obtainable on the basis of compensated reciprocity.

"Interpreting a just desire of public opinion, and without any wish to injure anyone, we ask that there be explained the grounds for the admission of the last contingent of immigrants that the vessel 'Iberia' brought to our port. If, as we would like to believe, none of the current requirements has been omitted, there should be no reluctance to making clear the fact in this case, so that we may all know what to expect in the future."

Failing to receive any response to its request for an explanation, the "Diario de la Marina" on January 29 again took up the matter:

"Contrary to what for obvious reason was to be expected, there has been no explanation of the underlying reason for the admission of the last contingent of Hebrews that arrived on the German vessel 'Iberia'.

- - - - - - - -

"There is ...... a reason of an international character that also requires that this be explained. It is that there has been permitted the entry of hundreds of Hebrews while thousands of Spaniards have been compelled to

leave

leave the country because of the nationalization of labor law, which was disgraceful and
inhuman at least for those who had acquired
families here; and there followed the expatria-
tion en masse, at the expense of the Government,
of Antilleans who had come in response to the
request of the sugar cane growers and with
previous official authorization, and the repatriation of these cannot be based upon a
surplus of labor if immigrants are being admitted meanwhile. How can such a thing be
justified should diplomatic claims be estab-
lished¿

"The invasion of Israelites has to be
curtailed drastically, all of whom, or in the
great majority, come to carry on trade or
manufacturing and so intensify the crisis. .....

"With what right can it be pretended that
we should accept more Hebrew refugees when
there are instances such as that which occurred
recently in Poland¿ Germany expelled, because
of the assassination of the third secretary of
the German embassy in Paris, ten thousand Polish
Jews, collecting them at Polish frontier sta-
tions, and the government at Warsaw, although
the matter concerned its nationals and it recognized that they would require urgent aid,
limited itself to resorting to the inter-govern-
mental commission functioning at London which
had under consideration assistance for the
persecuted of that race, requesting that it pro-
tect them since they could not return to the
place from which they came nor establish new
homes in their country of origin. If things
such as this happen, and all the great nations
that possess immense territories, including
imperial colonies, maintain restrictions and
haggle about the admission of Israelites, should
one as small as ours grant their admission, at
the risk of complicating still more its already
over-complicated problems¿"

On February 23 the Director General of Immigration

placed the following statement in the Habana newspapers:

"That he is decidedly favorable to closing
the ports of the country to all immigration
that intends to come to our territory to enter
into competition with native labor in any kind
of work, and under the circumstances he has not
authorized nor will he authorize in the future
the landing of any person, of any nationality
whatever, who intends to become a rival of our
compatriots, and that he takes very special care
that all who disembark fulfill the requirements

23

of

of current immigration regulations, and unless the applicant previously has declared
unequivocally that his journey here is solely
and exclusively to await the necessary visa
in order that he may enter the United States of
America or some other country where he can
locate permanently, that is, in the status of
a 'tourist'.

"That he knows perfectly the law of the
nationalization of labor and that he is disposed to give every cooperation that may be
necessary to the end that it shall not be
violated; that this, in addition to his obligation as an official, is his duty as a Cuban.

"That he is identified intimately with
the program of the Secretary of Labor to
assist the native and that he is disposed
to collaborate with that patriotic idea."

In another editorial, on March 6, "Diario de la

Marina" inquired, "Should we continue to receive more

alien refugees¿

"As everyone knows, the problem of
unemployment for some time has been very
grave in our country.

"The first measure adopted for the
purpose of solving it was the drastic law
of the nationalization of labor, as a result
of which thousands of aliens were left without employment, especially Spaniards, who
found themselves facing the dilemma of leaving
Cuba or dying of hunger.

"But contrary to what the government
responsible for this measure expected, it
did not remedy, even remotely, the unemployment situation, and in order to complete matters
there was instituted the repatriation en masse
of Antillean workers, which has not yet been
completed.

"Whether there is or is not still widespread unemployment, as stated, of infinitely
more eloquence than the figures of the census
of the same (1) is the fact that Cuba has been

converted

- -
(1) A recent newspaper ("El Mundo" - March 8, 1939) report
    stated that there are 500,000 unemployed in Cuba.

converted into a country of emigration (1), when
it always was one of immigration. That is to
say, now it is both, because emigrants leave
and immigrants enter, at the same time.

"Accordingly it can be asserted that there
is no decline in population, but an increase;
but nevertheless the country suffers from
serious afflictions. It suffers not only from
the ethnological and economic point of view,
because of the racial and occupational dif-
ferences between those who voluntarily leave
looking for something better, and those who
come in, protected by more or less deficient
requirements regulating immigration.

"In effect, the first are not only white
Cubans or Spaniards who are natives of the
Canary Islands and accordingly of our race, but
they are almost entirely agriculturists who
are betaking themselves from our country with
their families; on the other hand, the others,
who find it easy to enter without any requisite
other than a bond as a theoretical guarantee
that they will not become public charges, are
neither similar to us in any way nor do they
propose to contribute their resources to the
development of our agriculture.

"Unfortunately, neither in the country
nor in our cities is there today a scarcity
of labor. Quite the contrary, there is an
excess, as is being demonstrated not only by
the continual increase in unemployment in
spite of fruitless measures adopted to reduce
it, as we have previously stated, but also
and more evident, the emigration of families
that began two years ago and which is going
to increase if the economic condition of the
country fails to improve. Nevertheless, the
Government has not felt it necessary and useful to establish definite restrictions upon
the entry of immigrants. On the contrary, it
appears disposed to admit them in great
numbers."

25

After discussing the accomplishments of the confer-

ence at Evian, with emphasis upon the statements of the

representatives of Great Britain, France, Belgium, Nether-

lands, Canada, and the United States that such countries

are not prepared to admit large numbers of European

refugees

- -

(1) Several Cuban families have established themselves
    in an agricultural colony in Venezuela in the past
    two years and other Cubans have emigrated to the
    United States.

refugees, the Association for the Defense of Citizens
Rights inserted in "Diario de la Marina" of January
25, 1939, a lengthy article concerning immigration into
Cuba, from which the following excerpts are quoted:

> "It is worthwhile, in view of the delicate
> situation, to examine the question in its prin-
> cipal aspects, in order that Cuba as well as
> other Latin American countries may adopt in
> time the most urgent defense measures. The
> problem caused by the mass immigration of Jews
> expelled from Austria and Germany is comprised
> of three primary considerations:

> "The necessity that total annual migra-
> tions do not exceed the capacity of absorp-
> tion of the country; the desirability of es-
> tablishing quotas of immigration for countries
> and races in order that the population may
> preserve its traditional demographic charac-
> teristics; and the desirability of selecting
> immigrants by trades and occupations in order
> to avoid disturbing the national labor market.

> "The capacity of each country to absorb
> immigrants is limited. The nation is an
> organism whose economic and social necessities
> require careful attention. The entrance of
> great numbers of people in addition to what
> may be indicated, produces great disturbance
> and creates difficulties not less grave.
> Accordingly an immigration policy, generous
> and unlimited, which has been followed in
> some countries in our America, should be
> changed for one more selective in the States
> of less density of population.

- - - - - - -

> "But not only should there be avoided an
> excessive influx of people; it is necessary to
> watch carefully the quality of the human con-
> tingents called to be incorporated in our
> society. Migrations should not be by change
> nor should they take place at the political
> convenience of foreign governments. Cuba has
> the right to preserve its own characteristics,
> maintain its social traditions and safeguard
> its historic memories in the face of the cos-
> mopolitanism that invades it and the exoticism
> that weakens it, and accordingly there is an
> interest in keeping new immigrant contributions
> in proportion to the demographic basis of the
> country, avoiding the entrance on a large scale
> of ethnological elements difficult or undesirable

to

to assimilate. It is not possible to look with
indifference upon the old Spanish immigration,
which has been substituted in recent years for
another coming from Central and eastern Europe
(Poland, Lithuania, Rumania, Yugoslavia, Czecho-
Slovakia, etc.) with manners, principles and
ideas that already begin to appear in educational
centers, in cultural organizations, and in a
disturbing way in commercial and industrial centers.
The addition of large contingents of Jews would
accordingly increase at this time the accumulation
of racial elements that tend rapidly to denational-
ize and decharacterize the country.

"It is imperative to select immigrants more
carefully, as to trades and occupations, in order
that there be caused no serious disturbances in
the labor market by increasing unemployment and
paupers. In this respect the experience of the
past few years has been particularly painful
for merchants and manufacturers, by the invasion
of parasitic elements--small pedlers and hawkers--
who swarm over the entire city in ruinous competition and contributing to the low standard of
living of the native laborer. Accordingly, and
taking into account that the greater part of the
German and Austrian immigrants whose coming to
American the Intergovernmental Committee of London
advocates, are city people devoted to trade, it
is necessary to take defensive measures in order
that the situation through which national commerce
and industry are now passing, shall not be made
more acute.

"It should not be forgotten that the future
of Cuba is in its great and fertile lands, and
accordingly the only immigration that should be
advocated is that of agriculturists, provided
there are previously adopted necessary measures
for their distribution and there are organized
colonies useful in determining the zones of the
country.

"On the other hand, the admission of Jews
that has been reported, and of the good number
that have already entered, should not be considered while there exists in Cuba the Nationalization
of Labor Law, which has expelled from the country
or brought misery to thousands of Spanish for-
eigners with Cuban wives and children, who were
already incorporated in the national life, and
have given their energies during many years of
residence here, who came protected by the immigration laws then in effect, many of them re-
cruited by agents of the Government sent to
Spain to fill the requirements of the country.
A Law, in fact, that does not permit, under

penalty

27

penalty for the employer who violates it,
work for any alien while it is in effect."

Habana newspapers, and especially "Diario de la
Marina" which has been wholeheartedly anti-Nationalistic
in the Spanish civil war, also have expressed unreserved
disapproval of any efforts to permit Spanish nationalist
refugees in Spain to enter Cuba. In fact, it has been
proposed that the Cuban immigration regulations be
amended to provide for the exclusion of aliens of radical
beliefs. In this connection it was pointed out that Rus-
sia itself declined to accept the Spanish refugees in
France and that Mexico undoubtedly also would not do so.
It has been intimated that Cuba already has sufficient
of the communistic element in its own population. Undoubtedly the danger of immigration from Spain is but
another angle of the entire immigration problem ~~concerning~~
which the Cuban Government sooner or later will find it
necessary to meet by defining a more definite policy with
regard to all immigrants. While a large part of the population of Cuba not unnaturally has been sharply divided
in sympathy between the two opposing factions in the
Spanish struggle, the entry into this country of any
large number of active participants on either or both
sides undoubtedly would transplant here the seeds of
disturbance of concern not only to Cuba but to ourselves.

Decree No. 55 has been opposed in some respects by
the Cuban Chamber of Commerce, but its most pertinent
suggestion appears to be an inquiry as to whether the
cash bonds required of immigrants and which must be

deposited

deposited in the Postal Savings Bank "are to remain on deposit in the Postal Savings Bank or whether they are going to be loaned to government employees". (Special provision is made for the loan of Postal Savings Bank deposits to employees of the Cuban Government.) Whether or not their cash deposits will be returned to them should the conditions of their bonds be fulfilled is a matter that has occurred to refugees admitted in that manner, and is one reason why many are stated to prefer to pay outright an unofficial fee of $150 rather than risk the loss of $500.

This decree also has been opposed by the monthly Habana journal "Cuba Economica y Financiaera", which (February, 1939 issue) alleges that since the provisions of the decree modify a law, only the Congress may legislate such changes. It is held that the requirement regarding passport visas is unconstitutional for the reason that the Constitution provides that "Every person may enter the territory of the Republic, leave it, travel within its limits, and change his place of residence, without a letter of security, passport or other similar requirement, except what is provided in the laws regarding immigration and the authority granted to officials in case of criminal responsibility". This publication also maintains that the $500 cash bond is contrary to law, since a Military Order of 1899 having the force of law provides that "every cash bond required by the national, provincial or municipal governments and by the courts shall be substituted by bonds issued by bonding companies authorized by the laws". Decree No. 55 is held not to be in the best

29

interests

interests of Cuba since the country has only a population
of 4,000,000 "while its territory is capable of supporting
without difficulty from 15,000,000 to 20,000,000 inhabitants,
judging from the density of population in other countries
of similar area that enjoy relative prosperity".

> "Accordingly we should not fail to take
> into account that the basis of the progress of
> a Nation depends upon the population of its
> soil, the increase in the number if its inhabi-
> tants being the most decisive indication of the
> degree of its prosperity, for the density of
> population indicates capacity of its consumption,
> activity of its agriculture, its industry and its
> commerce, larger tax returns, greater exploita-
> tion of its potential production, and a higher
> grade of civilization."

It is known that the present Secretary of Labor does
not agree with the contention that Cuba does not now have
as large a population as the country can support. But
whether his opposition to the entry of aliens is based
upon a well-founded belief that this country for all time
has the maximum population it can support or whether it
is based only upon the more immediate and pressing desire
to alleviate unemployment existing at the present time,
it does not seem likely that his cooperation may be
expected in providing a refuge in this country for any
number of European refugees. Domestic political considerations also enter into the matter.

- - - - - - - - - - -

File No. 811.11/855

HST/jml

Distribution:
  Original and four copies to the Department;
  One copy to the Embassy.

DEPARTMENT OF STATE

DIVISION OF LATIN-AMERICAN AFFAIRS

MEMORANDUM

4/6/39.

Mr. Briggs:

This is a complete report from the Habana Consulate General on the handling of refugees in Cuba. About 2,500 refugees are now in Cuba. 300 of them are on relief (Habana Relief Committee). About $10,000 a month is sent to Cuba from the U.S. for the support of the others. From 1800 to 2000 of the total are expected to seek entry to the U.S. This refugee colony has developed within the past 7 months. About 500 more are arriving every month, which may continue as long as the Cuban requirements remain as they are.

The main features of technical procedure in the Cuban immigration service came to

---

DEPARTMENT OF STATE

DIVISION OF LATIN-AMERICAN AFFAIRS

MEMORANDUM

-2-

your attention the other day in connection with a letter from Ambassador Wright to Albert F. Coyle. (It seems to me that the word "confidential" might well have appeared in this instruction to London).

DIVISION OF THE AMERICAN REPUBLICS

31

To the American Ambassador,

London.

The Secretary of State encloses, for the information of the Vice Director of the Intergovernmental Committee on Political Refugees, a copy of a report from the American Consulate General at Habana, Cuba, dated March 18, 1939, concerning European refugees in Cuba.

32

MAR 30 1939. PM

Enclosure:

As stated.

Eu:SM:EMC
3-29-39

RA

Coert du Bois, Esquire,

American Consul General,

Habana, Cuba.

Sir:

The Department has received Mr. Tewell's strictly
confidential report entitled "European Refugees in Cuba"
completed on March 17, 1939. The report discusses in a
comprehensive manner a subject of great interest to the
Department at this time. Mr. Tewell should be commended
for his initiative in the submission of this thorough and
timely report which has been given the rating of "Excellent".

Very truly yours,

For the Secretary of State:

G. S. Messersmith

33

A true copy of
the signed origi-
nal.

837.55J/1

VD:JFH:MLS
4/11   FP   RA

May 1, 1939

My dear Mr. Houghteling:

I am enclosing for your strictly confidential
information a copy of an interesting report recently
received from the American Consul at Habana, Cuba,
concerning European refugees in Cuba.

Sincerely yours,

A. M. Warren
Chief, Visa Division

34

Enclosure:
Report.

James L. Houghteling, Esquire,
Commissioner of Immigration and Naturalization,
Department of Labor.

VD:MM:MLS
5/1

V O L U N T A R Y

S T R I C T L Y   C O N F I D E N T I A L

No. 344

EUROPEAN REFUGEES IN CUBA

(Supplementing reports of March 17,
April 1 and 19, 1939)

From:

Harold S. Tewell
American Consul

American Consulate   Date of Completion: May 9, 1939
General,   Date of Mailing: May 11, 1939
Habana, Cuba.

Approved:

Coert du Bois,
American Consul General.

File No. 811.11/855

HST/jw

Distribution:
    Original and four copies to the Department;
    One copy to the Embassy.

Entry of Jewish Refugees

Habana newspapers of May 4 (Diario de la Marina) contained the following news item:

"In Habana shipping circles there have been received reports that there is being organized in Europe an expedition of more than a thousand Jews, which will leave from a German port the middle of this month. It will arrive the early part of June.

"Many Hebrews who reside in Habana have received letters from their relatives and friends stating that they now have found a vessel on which they can come, there being many steamship companies that do not sell passages if they do not have previous authorization to disembark in Cuba.

"Officially nothing is known in the Immigration Department concerning the expected arrival of the thousand Jews. That office, moreover, in accordance with the law, does not have the power to authorize such immigration, especially since Mexico and the United States have indicated that they are opposed to their admission. Those Hebrews can be admitted to Cuba only as transients, to await here a visa to enter the United States and Mexico, something it is improbable they will get at this time.

"The Department of Labor, aware of the anticipated arrival of those thousand Hebrews, proposes to intervene, since there are denouncements that those passengers get to disembark as transients without filing a bond, by means of an affidavit, and once they land they look for and obtain work, displacing Cuban workers."

There also appeared in Habana newspapers an advertisement of the Hamburg American Line stating that the vessel "St. Louis" of 25,000 tons (instead of the smaller motor vessel "Iberia") will be in Habana the latter part of May, and a further news item states that on the "St. Louis" will arrive "one thousand Hebrew refugees".

It

It is understood that the refugees in question,
and perhaps many more who are not planning to travel
to Cuba on the vessel "St. Louis", have received letters or certificates signed by the Cuban Director
General of Immigration classifying them as tourists
and authorizing "entry and stay in Cuba for such
time as may be necessary to obtain a visa to enter
the United States of America or any other country",
provided the applicant "is not ill or physically
defective, that he has a passport, and that he does
not come to engage in work of any kind". The letter
or certificate states that classification as a tourist is granted in accordance with the provisions of
paragraph (a) of Article IV of Decree No. 55 of January 13, 1939, and Article 3 of Decree No. 2507 of
November 17, 1938. (See enclosures to report of
March 17, 1939).

Paragraph (a) of Article IV of Decree No. 55
provides that tourists (those who travel for pleasure
and do not work while in Cuba) are exempt from the
$500 bond required of foreigners entering this coun-
try, while Article 3 of Decree No. 2507 provides that
tourists are exempt from obtaining a passport visa,
which is required of "every alien desiring to be admitted to Cuban territory, temporarily or permanently.."

The newspaper article quoted above probably is
quite correct in stating that the Cuban immigration
department officially knows nothing concerning the

expected

37

expected arrival in Habana of one thousand Jewish refugees in one group. It is understood that the Director General of Immigration has not issued in his official office letters or certificates authorizing tourist status for such refugees, but that such letters have been issued in a private office maintained by him, upon payment of an unofficial fee of as much as $150 for each such document.

As stated in a report on this subject dated March 17, 1939, "the Director General of Immigration is handling the admission of European refugees largely according to his own inclination", since conflict between the Departments charged jointly with the enforcement of Decree No. 55 (State, Treasury and Labor) appears to have been instrumental in preventing the promulgation of regulations to carry out the provisions of that Decree.

In newspaper editorials and over the radio the continued admission of Jewish refugees has been severely criticized, and Habana newspapers on May 3 announced that a leading member of Congress had requested the President to promulgate a decree "prohibiting repeated immigrations of Hebrews who have been inundating the Republic and prohibiting permits that are being issued for the entrance of such immigrants to Cuba, until the House can approve a proposed law imposing severe penalties upon fraudulent immigration that makes a joke of the laws of the Republic".

The

The impasse that resulted from friction between various departments of the Government appears to have been removed, however, in Decree No. 937, which was issued on May 5 and published in the "Gaceta Oficial" on the same date. This measure, which is justified on the ground that "the modification of some existing regulations is desirable", greatly curtails the authority of the Director General of Immigration. A copy of the provisions of the decree is attached. The effect of these changes may be summarized as follows:

1. All aliens (except those who are likely to become public charges, who are excluded) must file bonds of five hundred pesos and permission for such aliens to disembark in Cuba shall be approved only by the Secretaries of State and Labor, which approval shall be issued in writing and sent direct to the transportation line concerned before the aliens may embark for Cuba in a foreign port. Heretofore this matter has been entirely in the hands of the Director General of Immigration, who is under the jurisdiction of the Treasury Department.

2. While transit passengers (those who remain in Cuba only while their vessel is in port) and transients (those who enter Cuba for not more than 30 days for the purpose of taking passage to another country or who return to the original port of departure) continue to be exempt from the $500 bond requirement imposed by Decree No. 55 of January 13, 1939, the only tourists exempt

without

39

without qualification from the bond requirement are
American citizens. Tourists of other nationalities may
be exempt from filing a bond if authorized in writing
by the Secretaries of State and Labor. Heretofore
bonds have not been required of any tourists and the
classification of aliens as tourists has been entirely
in the hands of the Director General of immigration.

3. All aliens who are required to post bonds and
obtain from the Secretaries of State and Labor written
authorization to land in Cuba, also must obtain passport visas, which may be granted only upon the authorization of the Departments of State and Labor. Heretofore the State Department alone was authorized to
approve the granting of visas, after consulting the
Departments of the Treasury and Labor. The modified
regulations accordingly give greater authority to the
Department of Labor in visa matters, while the function
of the Treasury Department (i.e. the Immigration Bureau)
continues to be only advisory in character.

4. While masters of vessels have been required to
report to port authorities the names of transit passengers remaining in Cuba, and steamship lines have
been held responsible for the return passage of rejected or deported aliens, the new regulations make transportation lines responsible for all expenses, including the cost of return passage, incurred in the case
of transit passengers and transients, and all aliens
who are brought to Cuba without complying with all re-

quirements

quirements of the immigration regulations. Provision
is made for legal measures to enforce this obligation.
It is not improbable that transportation lines bringing European refugees to Cuba have cooperated with the
Director General of Immigration in facilitating the
influx of such refugees into this country.

If the regulations set forth in Decree No. 937
are enforced it is clear that the Director General of
Immigration has been shorn of practically all authority respecting the entry of tourists as well as immigrant aliens. In the joint jurisdiction of the Secretaries of State and Labor have been placed the ac-
tual control of the admission of all non-immigrant
aliens except transit passengers, transients, and American tourists, and of all aliens of the immigrant class,
by means of requirements concerning visas and disembarkation permits. Whether this change in jurisdiction
implies a reduction in the entry of refugees from Europe, remains to be seen. It may be noted also that the
provisions of Decree No. 937 enable the Secretary of
Labor to attain an objective long sought by him, viz.,
greater control over immigration and aliens.

Spanish Refugees

From funds recently appropriated by the Cuban Congress arrangements recently were made to repatriate 185
of the 400 Cubans who served in Spanish loyalist armies
and who now are in concentration camps in France.
While organizations formed for that purpose have been

urging

urging the Government also to repatriate about 1,000 women and children who are stated to be destitute in Spain as a result of the war, newspaper reports indicate that attention first will be given to refugees in France, who are stated to face possible service in the French army should hostilities break out in Europe.

On May 6 General José Miaja, formerly of the Spanish loyalist armies and military commander of Madrid, arrived in Habana with his family, and accompanied by the following: his aide, José Gonzalez Burcet; the former Subsecretary of the Treasury, Mariano Sanchez Roca; former militia adjutants Julian Martinez Barrios, Juan Bornet Yopiz, Antonio Lopez Campa, Dr. Luis Fumagalli, and his secretary, Captain Antonio Lopez Fernandez. General Miaja was welcomed by a group of about 2,000 persons (according to newspapers) including the Mexican Consul, who was present upon instructions from his Government. It is understood that the General has been offered a position in a Mexican military school, but he is reported as saying that for the time being he will remain in Habana. Concerning the status of General Miaja, the Habana daily newspaper "El Mundo" (which was not noticeably partisan in the Spanish struggle) observed on May 7:

> "It is preferable, therefore, to remember only one thing: that General Miaja is our guest and that everyone, Cubans and Spaniards residing in Cuba, is obliged to be respectful and deferential toward one who has not hesitated to take refuge in our traditional hospitality."

While Decree No. 937 appears to strengthen the requirements of immigrants entering Cuba originally set

forth

forth in Decree No. 55 of January 13, 1939, it also provides for the repeal of any measures in conflict with the provisions of Decree No. 937. It is not understood, however, that the latter provision is construed as repealing Decree No. 767 of April 10, 1939 (See report of April 19, 1939), which declared that Decree No. 55 as then in force was "highly restrictive in that it is desirable to decrease competition with native manual labor, and prevents entry into the Republic of elements favorable to our nationality without complicated procedure". Accordingly, certain aliens entitled to "diplomatic courtesy" and aliens "who resided in Cuba several years and have here interests requiring their personal attention; and in exceptional cases, relatives of Cubans that reside abroad" still may be granted permission to enter Cuba under the loosely-defined procedure outlined in Decree No. 767. On April 20 the Secretary of State informed newspaper reporters (Diario de la Marina, April 21) that in such cases there should be presented to him application for a passport visa accompanied by a sworn statement setting forth the relationship of the alien to the applicant, proof that the former resided in Cuba for some years and that he has here interests that require his personal attention, a guarantee that the alien will not become a public charge or violate the labor laws, a guarantee that he will leave Cuba at the applicant's expense upon the expiration of the entry permit for one year, and proof that the alien "has complied with the immigration laws".

Regulations

43

Regulations applying to Decree No. 937

Since the foregoing material was prepared the Direct-
or General of Immigration has issued regulations to carry
out the provisions of Decree No. 937, which are quoted as
follows:

First: No person covered by the provisions of
Decree No. 937 of 1939 may be authorized to disembark
in Cuba without the permission of the Secretaries of
State and Labor, and in addition without the special
permission of this Bureau, which will verify whether
all the legal requirements issued by this Bureau
have been complied with, and without which the immigration authoriteis will not permit disembarkation.

Disembarkation permits issued by this Bureau in
Accordance with its authority and in accordance with
the provision of Decrees No. 55 and No. 2507 prior to
May 6, 1939, the date of Decree No. 937, will be valid
but from this date none will be issued unless applicants first obtain the required permission of the Secretaries of State and Labor.

Second: The shipping companies should transmit
with all urgency to their principal offices the provisions of Decree No. 937 and the instructions of
this Bureau in order that they may be carried out by
the said companies and avoid difficulties with the
Cuban authorities.

The immigration authorities will refuse the
right to disembark in Cuba to every person that appears to have not complied with the requirements of
laws as modified by Decree No. 937 and in every case
in which there is proved a violation of the legal
requirements by a steamship company, without delay
there will be initiated the legal action referred to
in Article V of Decree No. 937 in order to make effective the imputable responsibilities of the steamship company."

Although it appears that the Director General of Immigration henceforth will not issue to European refugees
in advance of their arrival, letters permitting them to
enter Cuba and will not permit them to land unless the
Secretaries of State and Labor previously have issued
disembarkation permits, the Director General himself will

not

not permit disembarkation until he is satisfied that all lagal requirements imposed by his office, have been complied with. In other words, many refugees may find it necessary to spend considerable time in the immigration detention station unless they deem it desirable to pay an unofficial fee for the Director General's disembarkation permit although the Secretaries of State and Labor may have previously issued such a permit as far as they are concerned.

It appears, moreover, that landing permits that have already been issued to regugees who have not yet arrived in Cuba, will be honored. There is no indication of the number of such landing permits that may have been issued to refugees who have not yet arrived in Cuba, but there is reason to believe that they may exceed in number the landing permits issued to the one thousand refugees that are expected to reach Habana the latter part of May.

According to Habana newspapers of May 10, steamship lines, especially European lines whose vessels call at Habana, have protested to the Treasury Department concerning the provisions of Decree No. 937, on the ground that such provisions restrict immigration from Europe and impose heavy obligations on such lines for violation of the Decree. It is stated also that representatives of foreign governments in Cuba also have complained, and as a result instructions have been given to the Treasury Department's legal advisors to study the matter and suggest any advisable modifications of the Decree.

It

45

It should be noted that the provisions of Decree No. 937 also apply to American steamship lines that transport to Cuba from the United States aliens who have been temporarily in the United States and who desire to come to this country to obtain immigration visas.

File No. 811.11/855

HST/jw

Distribution:
  Original and four copies to the Department;
  One copy to the Embassy.

46

DECREE NO. 937

(Published in Gaceta Oficial of May 5, 1939)

First: Article II of Decree No. 55 of January 13, 1939, will be rewritten as follows:

"Article II. Aliens not included in the prohibition established in the previous article and in any other shall be authorized to disembark in the national territory only upon filing a bond of five hundred pesos.

"This authorization will have to be granted personally, if approved by them, by the Secretaries of State and Labor, and communicated directly and in writing by those officials to the transportation companies, prior to the embarkation of the authorized (person) at the port of origin."

Second: Provision (a) of Article IV of the said decree will be rewritten as follows:

"A) Only tourists who are American citizens, that is, those persons of that nationality who travel for pleasure and are not engaged in any work during their stay in national territory. Tourists of other nationality only will have to obtain the authorization that is referred to in the second paragraph of Article II, without the necessity of filing any bond."

Third: The second paragraph of provision (c) of Article IV of the said decree will be rewritten as follows:

"The captain of the ship and consigners of the same will be obliged to inform the port authorities and the Secretaries of State, Treasury, and Labor concerning those passengers that may disembark in transit and to remain in the national territory.

"Transportation companies whose passenger lists include transients, will be obliged to inform the port authorities and the Secretaries of State, Treasury, and Labor, if, after thirty days from their arrival in Cuban territory, the transients have not embarked."

Fourth: Article IV of the said Decree 55 will be modified by the addition of the following paragraph:

"Transportation companies that bring passengers destined for Habana and other points in the Republic will be obliged, upon the arrival of their

respective

respective vessels, to send to the Departments of
State, Treasury, and Labor, a report in detail
concerning the name of each passenger and the place
whence he came; and upon leaving port, another report in which there is set forth the passengers
that continue the voyage, calling attention to
those that may not have done so, and consequently
who may have remained in the national territory."

Fifth: Article V of Decree 2507 of November 17,
1938, published in the Gaceta Oficial of the 20th of
that month, will be rewritten in the following form:

"Article V. Diplomatic and consular officers
of the Republic will report all cases of aliens
who, being obliged to make the deposit and obtain
the authorization to disembark in accordance with
immigration requirements, intend to come to Cuba;
and they will indicate the profession or occupation in which such aliens habitually are engaged,
and in those cases only will they perform the
visa service previously authorized by the Departments of State and Labor after consulting the
Treasury Department, and without which requisites
such a visa will be void.

"As a requisite for a visa of the passports
of aliens who are not American citizens who come
to Cuba and who are included in parts (d) and (e)
of Article lV of Decree No. 55 of 1939 and to
grant a visa it will be necessary that the diplomatic or consular officer be authorized to do so
by the Secretary of State, the entrance to the
national territory of those aliens having been
authorized by the Secretary of the Treasury, with
the approval of the Secretary of Education, in
cases which are covered by those two provisions."
(Refers to lecturers, scientists and clergymen.)

Sixth: Transportation companies that bring to the
national territory aliens covered by the immigration regulations, without complying with all requirements indicated therein, will be responsible for the expenses
incurred by such violators during their stay in Cuba
as well as for re-embarkation, and that responsibility
will be exacted of them by the Department of the Treasury by administrative judicial means, action being initiated by it officially or following denouncement by
the Departments of State or Labor.

The same responsibilities will be incurred by transportation companies with regard to passengers in transit
who remain in national territory, and companies that may
have granted passage from Cuba to a foreign place to
transients who have not embarked for the point of destination within thirty days from their arrival in national
territory.

Seventh

Seventh: The Secretaries of State, Treasury, and Labor are charged with the enforcement of this Decree with regard to the provisions that concern each.

Eighth: There are repealed such decrees, regula-tions, agreements and rules that conflict with the re-quirements of the provisions of this Decree, which will become effective on the date of its publication in the Gaceta Oficial of the Republic.

Done in the Presidential Palace, in Habana, May 5, 1939.

Translated: HST

Copied: jw

No. 760

To the American Ambassador,

    London.

    The Secretary of State encloses, for the strictly
confidential information of the Vice Director of the
Intergovernmental Committee on Political Refugees, a
copy of a voluntary report, dated May 11, 1939, from
the American Consulate General at Habana, Cuba, concerning European refugees in Cuba.

50

837.55 J/4

MAY 31 1939 PM

Enclosure:

    As stated.
Eu:SVCM:EMC
5-31-39

A true copy of
the signed origi-
nal.

iM/HM

NO. 1017

THE FOREIGN SERVICE
OF THE
UNITED STATES OF AMERICA

AIRMAIL

AMERICAN CONSULATE GENERAL
Habana, Cuba, June 7, 1939.

STRICTLY CONFIDENTIAL

SUBJECT: Jewish Refugee Situation in Habana.

ribution

THE HONORABLE

THE SECRETARY OF STATE,

WASHINGTON.

SIR:

I have the honor to submit the following report
regarding the situation in Habana created by the arrival from Europe on May 27 and May 28, 1939, of three
large transatlantic liners carrying an aggregate of
nearly 1300 Jewish refugees.

Legal and Illegal Background

The Department is aware from previous reports of
this office that for some time Colonel Benitez, Director
of Immigration in Habana, had been issuing landing permits in collusion with the Hamburg American Line which
were furnished to prospective passengers by the interested lines. An office was set up near the Hamburg
American Line passenger office in Habana where Colonel
Benitez is said to have issued several thousands of
these permits, over five thousand of which are still
outstanding. The factory price per permit was $160.
This was not an official fee and was not authorized by

law.

Doc. 3

51

law. It was an "unofficial" fee and presumably went
into Colonel Benitez' pocket. The Department's telegram
of May 27-3 P.M. - indicates that certain American groups
that had paid for landing certificates believed such pay-
ments to be legitimate charges and that delivery of the
service paid for could be demanded and presumably enforced.
The illegitimacy of the collections and the magnitude
of the sums collected are the crux of the whole "SAINT
LOUIS incident".

The landing permit purports to be issued pursuant
to Section A, Article 4 of Presidential Decree No. 55
of January 15, 1939 and Paragraph 3 of Decree No. 2507
of November 17, 1938. The permit "authorizes the entry
and establishment in Cuba for all of the period necessary to obtain a visa to enter the United States or any
other country". Section A of Article 4 of Decree No. 55
enumerates the exemptions from bond requirements and
defines tourists. It reads:

> "(a) Tourists; that is, those persons
> travelling for pleasure and who do not en-
> gage in labor during their sojourn in this
> country."

Paragraph 3 of Decree No. 2507 exempts tourists
(turistas) from the preceding paragraphs, 1 and 2, of
the decree which provides that aliens desiring to be
admitted into Cuban territory, temporarily or permanently, must have passports issued by their governments
and visaed by Cuban consuls. The Benitez landing
permit, therefor, classified its bearer as a tourist,
permitted his entry into Cuba for an indefinite stay,
and exempted him from bond and visa requirements.

On

On May 5, 1939, Decree 937 became effective through
publication in the Official Gazette. This amended Article II of Decree No. 55 to provide that authorization
for aliens to disembark in Cuba must be obtained in
writing from the Secretaries of State and Labor by transportation companies prior to their embarkation at the
port of origin. The bond requirement was retained.

Section IVa of Decree 55 which defined tourists
was amended to exempt American citizen tourists only
from bond and visa requirements and to require Cuban
visas (but not bonds) of tourists of all other nationalities.

The claim of the faction in the Cuban government
which opposed the landing of the European passengers
was based upon their arrival after the effective date
of Decree 937 without passports, visas or the authorization of the Secretaries of State and Labor. It was
stated that the Hamburg American Line had been officially
and categorically informed before the SAINT LOUIS sailed
from Hamburg (which was on May 13, nearly a week after
the effective date of Decree No. 937) that the new
decree would be strictly enforced.

Personal and Political Background

The Director General of Immigration, Manuel
Benitez Gonzalez, was a Colonel in the Army in the
Machado Regime and was in charge of troops in Oriente
Province. His son, also named Manuel Benitez, was a
sergeant in the army and one of the leaders in the 1933

mutiny

53

mutiny in which Colonel Batista assumed the command.
Young Benitez stamped out a military counter-revolution
in Pinar del Rio by personally shooting the fomenter
and thus earned the gratitude of Colonel Batista. He
is now a Lieutenant Colonel and commands the 8th Regi-
ment (Infantry) with headquarters in Pinar del Rio.
Through his service and loyalty to Colonel Batista
his father, Colonel Benitez, the Director General of
Immigration, has been under the Army aegis and enjoyed
considerable prestige and immunity. Under it he has
flouted the immigration laws and amassed a personal
fortune variously estimated at from half a million to
a million dollars.

54

Vigorously opposed to him were Dr. J. M. Portuondo,
Secretary of Labor and Dr. Juan J. Remos, Secretary of
State. They and their subordinates drafted and obtained
the promulgation of Decree No. 937 which was intended
to break Colonel Benitez' strangle-hold on immigration
to Cuba. Both of them, and particularly Portuondo, who
is the more forceful, urged President Laredo Bru to
call a show-down on the arrivals of the steamships
"Orduña", "Flandres" and "Saint Louis" -- all of which
sailed for Cuba after the effective date of Decree 937
with passengers bearing only Benitez landing permits.

This, of course, was in effect taking direct issue
with Colonel Batista who was Colonel Benitez' patron
and protector. It came on the heels of other incidents
indicating friction between the President's Palace and
Camp Columbia -- notably the resignation of Dr. Remos

as

as Secretary of State which Colonel Batista announced
and the President failed to accept.

In the present instance, however, the Palace
forces had little to fear in the way of intervention
by Camp Columbia in Benitez' behalf because:

a newspaper campaign against the Jews
had prepared a backing of public opinion;

the sale of landing permits had been
too open and notorious and had netted such
huge sums; and

the violation of Cuban laws by foreign
steamship companies had been flagrant and
defiant.

Colonel Batista had a bad attack of the grippe
which confined him to his bed during the whole of the
SAINT LOUIS incident and, under doctor's orders, prevented him from even receiving any reports on current
happenings.

Negotiations for Landing the Refugees

As late as the evening of May 26, the day before
the SAINT LOUIS arrived, there was no reason to believe
that Colonel Benitez would not be able to make good on
his landing permits. He had made unequivocal statements to that effect and the opposing forces had not
yet shown the full strength of their hands. The Consulate General kept in close touch with the local office
of the Joint Relief Committee, in charge of Mr. W. D.
Goldsmith and Miss Laura Margolis, and kept the

Ambassador

55

Ambassador informed of every move.

On May 27 it was learned that President Laredo Bru had issued an order the night before, ordering the SAINT LOUIS to remain at anchor, to land no passengers, to permit no one aboard, and specifically forbidding Colonel Benitez or his men to go aboard or clear any passengers to Tiscornia. The events of the next few days are set forth in the enclosed copies of memoranda for the Embassy and for the files by which I have tried to keep a record of a rapidly changing and very complicated situation. The most important document is the Ambassador's memorandum of his conversation with Secretary of State Juan Remos which took place at the Ambassador's residence on the afternoon of Memorial Day and after the Ambassador and I had conferred most of the morning. This memorandum indicates clearly that the Ambassador felt that the humanitarian aspects of the situation were the only ones that might properly be stressed by the ranking representative of the United States.

My part in the events of the last few days has been to try to keep abreast of them; to keep the Ambassador and the Department informed; to put myself and what possibly useful local knowledge I might possess at the disposal of the American organizations working for the relief of these refugees and to advise and encourage, so far as possible, American relatives of these unfortunates who had come to Habana.

Very respectfully yours,

Coert du Bois
American Consul General

Enclosures:

Enclosures:

No. 1. Memorandum dated May 29, 1939 - "Telegrams
        referring to refugees . . ."
No. 2. Strictly Confidential memorandum dated May 29,
        1939 - "At 11:45 A.M. today the attached
        message was telephoned to Mr. Avra M. Warren,
        . . ."
No. 3. Memorandum from the Embassy dated May 30, 1939,
        of conversation between Dr. Juan J. Remos,
        Cuban Secretary of State, and the Ambassador.
No. 4. Strictly Confidential memorandum dated May 31,
        1939 - "At 4:00 P.M. Dr. Mario Lazo called
        and said that he had just had a telephone
        conversation with Mr. Ramos . . . ."
No. 5. Strictly Confidential memorandum dated May 31,
        1939, carrying over into June 1. - "At
        luncheon at the American Club on May 31 the
        Ambassador and the Consul General . . ."
No. 6. Strictly Confidential memorandum dated June 1,
        1939 - "At 1:30 P.M. Mr. Berenson called me
        at my house and said that he had just returned
        from an interview with the President. . . ."
No. 7. Strictly Confidential memorandum dated June 5,
        1939 - "At 11:25 A.M. today Avra M. Warren,
        . . . telephoned from Washington . . ."
No. 8. Strictly Confidential memorandum dated June 5,
        1939 -"At 12:30 P.M. on Saturday, June 3,
        1939 Miss Cecilia Razovsky called and said
        that Mr. Berenson . . . "
No. 9. Strictly Confidential memorandum for the Ambas-
        sador dated June 5, 1939, entitled "Jewish
        Refugees on the S.S. ST. LOUIS".
No.10. Strictly Confidential memorandum dated June 6,
        1939 - "At 9:30 P.M. last night, June 5,
        Berenson called my house and stated that he
        had tried but unable to telephone the Ambas-
        sador . . . "
No.11. Strictly Confidential memorandum dated June 6,
        1939 - "1:30 P.M. I have just had a talk
        with Mario Lazo . . ."
No.12. Strictly Confidential memorandum dated June 6,
        1939 - "At 1:30 P.M. today Berenson called
        me at the American Club and said he wanted
        to see me at once. . . ."
No.13. Strictly Confidential memorandum dated June 6,
        1939, carrying over into June 7 - "At 6:00
        P.M. today Berenson telephoned me at my
        house and said he had a matter of utmost
        urgency to discuss with me at once . . ."

57

File 811.11/855

CduB/jml

(Submitted in triplicate)
(Copy for the Embassy)

(Enclosure No. 1 to Despatch No. 1017, dated June 7, 1939, entitled "Jewish Refugee Situation in Habana" — American Consulate General, Habana, Cuba)

C O P Y

AMERICAN CONSULATE GENERAL
Habana, Cuba, May 29, 1939.

Telegrams referring to refugees on board the SAINT LOUIS will be replied to along the following lines:

"Acknowledging your telegram re European refugees on board steamer SAINT LOUIS please be assured Consulate General doing everything it properly can along the line of unofficial good offices. Humanitarian aspects of situation have been emphasized to Cuban Government. Department of State is being kept currently informed.

Du Bois, Consul General"

CduB

811.11-

CduB/jml

Copy for the Ambassador

(Enclosure No. 2 to Despatch No. 1017, dated June 7, 1939,
entitled "Jewish Refugee Situation in Habana"- American
Consulate General, Habana, Cuba)

C O P Y

AMERICAN CONSULATE GENERAL
Habana, Cuba, May 29, 1939

STRICTLY CONFIDENTIAL

MEMORANDUM FOR THE FILES

At 11:45 A.M. today the attached message was telephoned
to Mr. Avra M. Warren, Chief of the Visa Division, Department
of State, who read it to a stenographer and made it of record
in the Department.

After dictating the message I told Mr. Warren that the
Ambassador and I were in constant conference with regard
to the German refugee situation and that we would take no
action along the line of making representations to the Cuban
Government without first obtaining instructions for such
action from the Department. Mr. Warren said that he was
very glad I had brought this matter up as he had discussed
it with Mr. Welles, who was distinctly against the representatives of the State Department in Habana making representations to the authorities looking to the admission of
European aliens into Cuba. He said that the Jewish Relief
Committees in New York were bringing pressure to bear to
induce persons of the standing of Barney Baruch to telephone
to the President of the United States, urging him to have his
Government make representations to the Cuban Government looking to the entry of these aliens into Cuba. He said no
instructions along this line had come through from the
White House and he said further that we in Habana appeared
to be handling the situation very satisfactorily. I promised
to keep him posted of any change in the situation.

Coert du Bois
American Consul General

811.11-
CduB/jml
Copy for the Ambassador

(Enclosure No. 3 to Despatch No. 1017, dated June 7, 1939,
entitled "Jewish Refugee Situation in Habana" -
American Consulate General, Habana, Cuba)

Conversation   Dr. Juan J. Remos,
May 30, 1939   Cuban Secretary of
                                      State

                                      The Ambassador

                        ———

        During a conversation today with the Cuban
Secretary of State upon other matters, I improved
the opportunity to inquire informally as to the
present status of the German-Jewish refugees on
board the SS. St. LOUIS now in Habana harbor.
Doing so, I bore in mind the following facts: that
Consul General du Bois has been giving constant
and close attention to the matter of these refugees
as well as to the situation which was created by
the arrival of persons in a similar category on
the ORDUNA and the FLANDRE; he and I have been in
close communication since the situation first arose
in an endeavor properly to evaluate it and also
to keep abreast of developments in order that every
effort which is properly possible might be exerted;
that the Consul General had telegraphed a report
of the situation on the 29th instant to the Department of State in order to enable the Department to
answer such inquiries as might be forthcoming from
interested parties; and that the Consul General had
spoken by telephone to Mr. Avra Warren, Chief of
the Visa Section of the Department of State in
Washington, who had informed Mr. du Bois that the
Department of State desired that we make no official
representations to the Cuban Government in this
matter.

        I therefore made it as clear as possible to
the Secretary that my inquiries were prompted by
no instructions but merely in order that I might
be able to reply to the inquiries which had been
made of the Consulate General and of me by relatives
in the United States of the refugees concerned, as
well as by the persons who had subscribed to the
funds for their transportation and maintenance in
Cuba and by officials of the relief organizations.

        The Secretary said that he was deeply con-
cerned regarding the entire matter but that the
only factor in the situation which directly concerned his Department was whether Cuban consular
officers had properly fulfilled their functions
and discharged their duties in connection with
visas that may have been issued to persons bearing
legitimate passports and desirous of entering Cuba.
He said that he was well aware of the fact that
allegations have been made that certain Cuban
consular officers had acted irregularly, and that
an examination was being made of each of these cases.

                                              He

He then referred quite frankly to other irreg-
ularities in connection with this entire matter
and spoke without reserve of the pernicious practice
that has arisen by which Colonel Benitez, Director
of Immigration, had issued Immigration Permits upon
the payment of $160 per permit, which permits were
transmitted to the prospective immigrants by the
respective steamship lines and he stated that the
pursuance of such a practice could not but ultimately
be productive of trouble, complications and unpleasant
accusations. He said further that he had requested
the steamship lines not to sell tickets to persons
whose passports did not bear the necessary visa but
that apparently the steamship company (especially
the Hapag) had not observed this precaution - a
failure which contributed in large part to the
present complications. The Secretary went even so
far as to say that the issuance of such a number
of Immigration Permits at so high a price was
certainly a very good "negocio" and he clearly
indicated that the practice met with his disapproval.
I inquired whether he was aware of the fact that
these passengers - certainly on the SS. St. LOUIS,
if not on the other ships - were compelled to purchase round-trip tickets to be paid for in francs,
pounds, or dollars - and that in the case of the
Hapag passengers, restitution of the price of the
return portion of the ticket in case the passengers
were admitted to Cuba was to be made not in the
currency in which it was purchased but in blocked
Reichsmarks: the Secretary said that he was not
so aware.

Again emphasizing the fact that I was entirely
without instructions as to any representations what-
soever in this matter, I said that I still felt
very much alive to the humanitarian considerations
involved, although I desired to recall to his
attention the wording of the first circular telegram
of the President of the United States to all nations
regarding the refugee situation in which the President, while appealing to humanitarian considerations,
stated quite clearly that it was not proposed that
any nation be asked or expected to consent to admit
a greater number of aliens than that prescribed by
its legislation: the Secretary said he clearly
recalled this fact.

I then said that the matter which chiefly
concerned me was that unpleasant repercussions
would almost inevitably arise from the very practice to which he had himself referred: i.e., that
an official of the Cuban Government had issued
Immigration Permits to these refugees at the rate
of $160 per card - notwithstanding which they had
been denied admission to the country upon arrival

61

in

in Habana; whether such action was the result of intervening or retroactive legislation seemed to me to make little difference. It therefore seemed to me almost inevitable that these refugees, as well as those who had returned on the cruise which is previously mentioned, as well as friends, relatives and members of the relief committees, would lose little time in acquainting the press with the situation, in a manner which I feared might be most derogatory to the Government.

The Secretary said that he shared my apprehension in all these regards and that his personal opinion was that the persons now in Habana should be admitted - provided proper guarantees were given that they would not become public charges, that they would not replace any Cubans in everyday occupations and that other guarantees would be forthcoming by the appropriate committees and authorities that they would be maintained during their sojourn in Cuba and would ultimately proceed to their destination. I said that I thought that there would be little difficulty in obtaining assurances which would be satisfactory to the Cuban authorities - although I had no authorization or instructions whatever to say so. I added that I thought that additional precautions might well be taken in order to prevent a recurrence of such a situation: i.e., that the practice of issuing such immigration permits should be discontinued or, if it seemed necessary that this unusual practice be persisted in, such permits be only sold to those persons who had obtained the necessary visas; and, furthermore, that the steamship companies be directed to desist from accepting passengers who did not possess the necessary visas and, still further, that appropriate steps be taken to avoid the recurrence of similar difficulties in connection with the balance of the large number of Immigration Permits which had already been issued and paid for. The Secretary stated that he concurred in my observations and reiterated my understanding that I offered them informal good offices in a personal capacity without instructions, but in a desire to prove of assistance to his country.

The Secretary stated in closing that the matter would be discussed at a Cabinet meeting tomorrow and that meanwhile the departure of the SS. St. LOUIS would be delayed. I gained the impression that the awkwardness of the situation was becoming increasingly evident to Cuban Governmental authorities.

The Ambassador

JBW:hmc

(Enclosure No. 4 to Despatch No. 1017, dated June 7, 1939,
entitled "Jewish Refugee Situation in Habana" -
American Consulate General, Habana, Cuba.

C O P Y

AMERICAN CONSULATE GENERAL
Habana, Cuba, May 31, 1939

STRICTLY CONFIDENTIAL

MEMORANDUM FOR THE FILES

At 4:00 P.M. Dr. Mario Lazo called and said that he
had just had a telephone conversation with Mr. Ramos, Secretary of National Defense, who at the time was in a meeting with officials at Camp Columbia and could not speak
very clearly. He said that so far as the SAINT LOUIS was
concerned he was afraid it was a closed case (the phrase
was "caso cerrado"). He went on to tell Mario Lazo that
he would be glad to go into detail with regard to the
situation at his house in Miramar at 8:00 tonight either
with him alone or with the Ambassador, or with me. I
told him I thought it would be much better if he would
see Mr. Ramos alone and communicate the information to
the Ambassador or to me later.

On receiving this information I immediately called
the Ambassador who stated that it would be much better if
Mario Lazo saw Mr. Ramos alone. I had no sooner completed
my conversation with the Ambassador when Dr. Lazo phoned
again and said that Mr. Ramos had just called him a second
time and said that he was unable to communicate to him
what he wanted to say over the phone and that he would come
to Lazo's office if he desired, as he might have created a
false impression by what he said, because he meant "so
far as he was concerned". Mario Lazo said that he was
going out to Camp Columbia at once to see Ramos and would
inform me or the Ambassador at the Club after his interview

as to its results.

The Ambassador stated that it would be better to wait until all information was available before attempting to report to Washington, and then to do so by telephone.

Coert du Bois
American Consul General

811.11-General

CduB/jml

Copy for the Ambassador

64

(Enclosure No. 5 to Despatch No. 1017, dated June 7, 1939,
 entitled "Jewish Refugee Situation in Habana" --
 American Consulate General, Habana, Cuba.

AMERICAN CONSULATE GENERAL
Habana, Cuba, May 31, 1939

STRICTLY CONFIDENTIAL

MEMORANDUM FOR THE FILES

At luncheon at the American Club on May 31 the
Ambassador and the Consul General asked Mario Lazo if
he could tap any sources of information as to what trans-
pired at and what were the results of the protracted
meeting of the Cabinet today. About 4:00 P. M. Mario
Lazo called up and said that he had been out to Camp
Columbia to see Dr. Ramos, Secretary of Defense, who
told him that the Cabinet had voted unanimously to ex-
clude the Jewish refugees and require the SAINT LOUIS
to sail with all on board. He said that the humanitarian
aspects of the situation had been presented at the meeting by Ramos, Secretary of State, but that the President
was distinctly intransigeant. The President feels, apparently, that a lesson must be dealt to the Hamburg American
Line which had brought these passengers here with documents obtained through bribery after they had been categorically informed that passengers brought under such
circumstances would not be allowed to land. The Line
had deliberately slapped the President of the Republic
in the face. While the President felt deeply the pitiable
situation of the refugees he also felt so strongly that
this was an opportunity to end once and for all the
financial abuses that had developed between the Hamburg
American Line and the Cuban Immigration Service that to
send the ship back to Germany was the lesser of two evils.

Later

Later (5:40 P.M.) Mario Lazo came to the Club and corroborated verbally to the Ambassador and to the Consul General the foregoing report, and added that Dr. Ramos had said that the person whom the President held most responsible for this deplorable situation was Lawrence Berenson who had definitely been told several months ago that refugees arriving under the circumstances of those on the SAINT LOUIS would not be admitted. Evidently Berenson elected to disregard the warning and play the game of Colonel Benitez and the Hamburg American Line.

June 1, 1939

The morning papers carried a front page story under the headline "Hope is Seen for Homeless on SAINT LOUIS", in the first paragraph of which "it was reported in authoritative sources last night that 922 homeless European refugees aboard the S. S. SAINT LOUIS will be permitted to land in Cuba". In an effort to check this report the Consul General called up Mario Lazo who said that his informant of the previous day (Dr. Ramos) had just called him and said he had seen the report in the paper but he had had no word from any Government source to indicate the truth of it. He said, however, that he had not been in touch with the situation for the last few hours. He promised Mario Lazo to check in cabinet circles and find out what had happened, if anything, to justify the report. He was to call Mario Lazo back at 11:00 A. M. but at the time of his call he knew of no change in the situation from that of his conversation

with

with Mario Lazo the previous evening.

At 10:00 A. M. the Consul General called the Joint
Relief Committee office to ask Goldsmith what basis, if
any, there was for the newspaper story. The phone was
immediately taken by Berenson who reported as follows:
He had been in touch during the night with Lopez Castro
and Garcia Montes who had assured him that "Everything
was O. K. above". They two were to confer with the
President at 9:00 A.M. and were to present for the
President's consideration the guarantees that the Joint
Relief Committee was prepared to make in behalf of the
refugees. Colonel Mariné called him from Camp Columbia
at 4:45 A. M. this morning and told him the President
would see him in the Palace at 4:00 P.M. today. Later
this morning he had received a telephone message from
the Palace to the effect that the President would see
him at 12 Noon. He said that he felt very much encour-
aged and that he thought it was all over but the shouting,
since it was now simply a question of guarantees.

Coert du Bois
American Consul General

811.11-General

CduB/jml

Copy for the Ambassador

67

(Enclosure No. 6 to Despatch No. 1017, dated June 7, 1939,
entitled "Jewish Refugee Situation in Habana" --
American Consulate General, Habana, Cuba.

C O P Y

AMERICAN CONSULATE GENERAL
Habana, Cuba, June 1, 1939

STRICTLY CONFIDENTIAL

MEMORANDUM FOR THE FILES

At 1:30 P.M. Mr. Berenson called me at my house and said
that he had just returned from an interview with the President.
He said that he had attempted to point out to the President the
horrible plight of the people on the ST. LOUIS and the humanitarian principles involved, but that the President had inter-
rupted him to say that no one was more fully aware of or more
sympathetic with the situation than he but that he had to maintain the prestige of the Cuban Government viz-a-viz the Hamburg
American Line and that he had ordered the ship with all on
board out of the port of Habana as soon as it was able to get
up steam. He said that after the ship had left the port of
Habana and was outside territorial limits (meaning the three-
mile limit) he was willing to listen to any plan of guarantees
which might be offered covering their maintenance in Cuba until
such time as they could go elsewhere.

Mr. Berenson said that he put forward the Isle of Pines
idea. He said that Lopez Castro and García Montes had seen
the President this morning and had urged a favorable solution
and that when Colonel Mariné called him at 4:45 this morning
he, the Colonel, expressed the conviction that everything
would come out all right. Berenson's manner and tone were
encouraging, in other words, he seemed to believe that the
President meant what he said and that after he had saved his
face by having the ship leave the port, its passengers would

be

be allowed to return under satisfactory guarantees to the Isle
of Pines or elsewhere in Cuba--certainly not Habana.

I asked Berenson what kind of information was to be
given to the Press and he said he did not know. He said he
had asked the President to give some assurance to the Jewish
community and to the unfortunate people on the boat that the
deportation would not be permanent. Apparently the President
was non-committal on this subject. Berenson said further
that he had asked the President to authorize his visit to the
ST. LOUIS to allay the fears of the passengers--among whom he
feared a suicide wave. The President declined. Berenson
said that as he left the President's Palace he saw Colonel
Benitez, who looked very badly. He heard at the Palace that
Benitez had submitted his resignation but that the President
was still considering it. He said he was leaving the (Sevilla-
Biltmore) hotel at once and going out to the finca of Castro
Lopez (former Secretary of Agriculture) where they would meet
García Montes (present Secretary of Agriculture) and try and
frame a plan of "guarantees" satisfactory to all concerned.
He asked me to convey this information to the Ambassador, which
I did at 2:00 P. M. at the American Club.

3:30 P.M. Pilot's Association has no information re the
ST. LOUIS.

3:45 P.M. A prospective passenger from Habana to Spain on
the return trip of the ST. LOUIS states that it is reported
on the street that the President has signed a decree ordering the Hamburg American Line to get the ship out of the Port
inside of 24 hours or the Cuban Navy will take her out.

4:00 P.M.

69

<u>4:00 P.M.</u> Mario Lazo called and said he had heard from "another" source that the President was signing a decree ordering the ship out of the port. He was told in confidence my information from Berenson.

Coert du Bois
American Consul General

811.11-General

CduB/jml

Copy to the Ambassador

4:05 P.M. I telephoned a full verbal report on the developments of the last three days and the situation to date to Mr. Coulter, Assistant Chief of the Visa Division, Department of State, Warren being out.

CduB

70

(Enclosure No. 7 to Despatch No. 1017, dated June 7, 1939,
entitled "Jewish Refugee Situation in Habana"
American Consulate General, Habana, Cuba.

C C P Y

AMERICAN CONSULATE GENERAL
Habana, Cuba, June 5, 1939

MEMORANDUM FOR THE FILES

STRICTLY CONFIDENTIAL

At 11:25 A.M. today Avra M. Warren, Chief of the Visa
Division, Department of State, telephoned from Washington
and said that he had just had a telephone conversation with
the Joint Relief people in New York, who said that they understood that demands were being made on Berenson by the
Cuban Government for greatly increased bonds to guarantee
the SAINT LOUIS passengers and that they had heard that
guarantees of upwards of $250,000 would be demanded. They
said that the Maryland Casualty Company did not have this
amount of capital in Habana and had asked Warren's advice
as to whether some other form of guarantee with the money
in New York would not be acceptable to the Cuban Government,
and had asked his advice as to how they should act. He
wished me to advise him. I told him that I thought it would
be very much better not to offer any advice on this subject
and that they should consult with and get the advice of
their representative in Habana, Mr. Lawrence Berenson. I
then said that the best way I could acquaint him with the
situation was to read him a memorandum I had just dictated
for the files with regard to the meeting of the Ambassador,
Berenson and myself at my house last night. When I concluded,
Warren said "I get it. We will keep out of this".

71

Coert du Bois
American Consul General

811.11-General
CduB/jml
Copy for the Ambassador

(Enclosure No. 8 to Despatch No. 1017, dated June 7, 1939,
entitled "Jewish Refugee Situation in Habana"
American Consulate General, Habana, Cuba.

C O P Y

AMERICAN CONSULATE GENERAL
Habana, Cuba, June 5, 1939

MEMORANDUM FOR THE FILES

STRICTLY CONFIDENTIAL

At 12:30 P.M. on Saturday, June 3, 1939 Miss Cecilia
Razovsky called and said that Mr. Berenson, working in con-
junction with Mr. Castro Lopez and Mr. García Montes, had
evolved the following plan of settlement of the SAINT LOUIS
affair which was to be submitted to the President that afternoon.

A surety bond was to be offered by the Maryland Casualty
Company, which is authorized under Cuban law to do business
in Cuba, in the amount of $50,000 or more if necessary, to
cover for a period of six years a guarantee that the SAINT
LOUIS passengers would not become a public charge in Cuba
and would not violate any of the Cuban law laws. It provided that after three years all males over 21 years old
not occupied in productive and noncompetitive activities
were to be removed from the Island of Cuba and taken elsewhere at the expense of the Joint Relief Committee. In
return, the passengers of the SAINT LOUIS were to be landed
at once in Habana and the Committee was to be given nine
months in which to distribute them in various points in Cuba
and on the Isle of Pines. Educational and training centers
were to be started at the various points where these people
were settled and special arrangements were to be made for
the care and vocational training of the children. There

are

are reported to be 917 passengers on board the SAINT LOUIS,
of whom 540 were under 21 and over 25 years old, leaving
only some 365 who might be in a position to compete with
Cuban labor.

Miss Razovsky told a long and complicated tale of
(Berenson's) being pursued from place to place during most
of Friday night by Major Bernardo García and Colonel Benitez,
Batista's aide from Camp Columbia and son of the defaulting
Director of Immigration. It was assumed by Berenson that
these two officers had some graft proposition to make and
therefore he did his best to keep clear of them. He was run
to earth in his hotel room about 3:00 A.M. where young Benitez
made a sort of set speech expressing Colonel Batista's re-
grets in the recent occurences and the inability of the
Cuban Government to make good on the Benitez landing permits,
and then he went away. It was evident that he was obeying
orders and that he had been sent to apologize for his
father's actions.

As regards the Santo Domingo idea, Miss Razovsky did
not seem to take it very seriously. She said that the first
it had been broached to Berenson was at 10:30 Saturday
morning, when Nestor Pou, Consul of the Dominican Republic
in Habana, came to see Berenson at the Sevilla-Biltmore
Hotel and said that his Government was prepared to receive
the SAINT LOUIS passengers and would not adhere strictly
to its requirement for a $500 cash bond for the entry of
each alien, but was willing to listen to any sort of a
guarantee that the Joint Relief Committee wanted to make
covering the entire group on the SAINT LOUIS.

At

73

At 10:30 A.M., Sunday, June 4th, the Ambassador called
me at my home and said that Berenson had gotten him on the
telephone at a party at the Aguilar's house about midnight
the preceding night and had talked for nearly an hour about
the SAINT LOUIS situation. He said that apparently the
President was going to accept the plan as outlined to me
by Miss Razovsky, with certain unimportant modifications,
one being that the surety bond should be for $150,000 rather
than $50,000, but that the period covered should be 9 years
instead of 6 years, and that all males over 21 years of age
should be moved out of the country as soon as possible.
Another modification was that the ship should land its
passengers at Matanzas instead of Habana.

At 9:00 P.M., Sunday, June 4th, the Ambassador called
again and said that Berenson had just gotten him on the
phone in great distress and wanted to see him and me immediately, for advice. He did not want us to come to the
Embassy, so I suggested that both come to my house. They
both came at 9:30 and Berenson told us of his difficulties
until nearly midnight. It seems now that the negotiators
on the part of the President, Ochotorena and Bernardo
García, and the President himself, insist that all of the
guarantees mentioned in the plan outlined above must be
in addition to the regular cash bond of $500 for each
individual alien on board the SAINT LOUIS. This involves
a deposit in the Cuban Treasury of some $450,000, which
must be made immediately or the SAITN LOUIS would continue
on to Germany. As a matter of fact, Clasing of the Hamburg
American had served notice to Bustamante that he could
keep the ship hanging around West Indian waters for only

74

24 hours longer, which would be 4:00 P.M., June 5th. It
seems also that Bustamante, the Joint Relief Committee
lawyer in Habana, has double-crossed his employers and is
now advising the President and his advisers to insist on
the $500 cash bond requirement. In other words, Berenson's
house of cards, so painfully and carefully built up, seems
to have fallen down. The advice that Berenson obviously
wanted the Ambassador and me to give him was to go personally
to Colonel Batista and get him to instruct the President to
accept the surety bond plan and waive the individual cash
bonds. He got no such advice. The Ambassador and I urged
Berenson to get in touch at once with Clasing and find out
definitely and authoritatively where the SAINT LOUIS was
and how long it could be kept in these waters. We then
suggested strongly that he give serious consideration to
the Santo Domingo offer and get in touch again with Mr. Pou,
the Dominican consul. It was evident that Berenson himself
was very reluctant to accept the Santo Domingo solution
and that he believed his principals in New York would also
be. Although he was repeatedly asked the reason for this
reluctance, he was exceedingly vague in his replies. It
was pointed out to him that the Santo Domingo scheme was
his ace in the hole, and it seemed that the time had come
to play it.

75

Coert du Bois
American Consul General

811.11-General
CduB/jml

Copy to the Ambassador

C O P Y

AMERICAN CONSULATE GENERAL
Habana, Cuba, June 5, 1939

STRICTLY CONFIDENTIAL

MEMORANDUM FOR THE AMBASSADOR

Jewish Refugees on the S. S. ST. LOUIS

The Consulate General has been given the following information by a source that is believed to be reliable concerning the landing in Cuba of Jewish refugees on the vessel SAINT LOUIS.

The President has proposed to permit the landing of these refugees upon the delivery of $150,000 in cash (termed a bond) under the following conditions:

1. He will not deal directly with Berenson or with Bustamante (for obvious reasons).

2. Arrangements must be made by the Jewish agencies through the representative of the President, who is stated to be one Emilio Pino Redondo in the first place, and a lawyer named Cueto in the second place, the latter being the one designated to deal directly with the Jewish agencies.

3. A $500 cash bond must be deposited with the Cuban Government for each refugee, and this amount will be retained until the alien leaves Cuba, or if he decides to remain permanently or indefinitely, the bonds would be refunded to the depositors in instalments, as they demonstrate that they are not public charges.

4. The SAINT LOUIS may not again enter Habana with these passengers, but if the above terms are met, arrangements

have

have been made to land them at Cienfuegos (the President's home city), where it is said that merchants and other business people would welcome the influx of a population with money to spend. It is stated that arrangements also have been made to obtain sufficient living quarters in Cienfuegos for the number of refugees involved. Alternatively, they may land on the Isle of Pines, but whether they land at Cienfuegos or on the Isle of Pines, the refugees may not leave that particular community without permission.

5. The President stipulated that if his proposal was not accepted by noon on June 2 he would issue an order that the SAINT LOUIS leave Habana, but it is stated that the President's ultimatum has been worded in such a manner that his proposal still stands if the Jewish agencies are inclined to negotiate through the channels indicated.

6. It is stated that the Hamburg- American Line has offered to match any sum the Jewish relief agencies might contribute in arranging the landing of the SAINT LOUIS passengers.

77

Coert du Bois
American Consul General

811.11-General

HST/jml

(Enclosure No. 1C to Despatch No. 1017, dated June 7, 1939,
entitled "Jewish Refugee Situation in Habana" --
American Consulate General, Habana, Cuba.

AMERICAN CONSULATE GENERAL
Habana, Cuba, June 6, 1939

MEMORANDUM FOR THE FILES

STRICTLY CONFIDENTIAL

At 9:30 P.M. last night, June 5, Berenson called my
house and stated that he had tried but was unable to telephone the Ambassador. He said that he wished to report that
that evening a conference was being held between President
Laredo Bru, Colonel Batista, and Major Bernardo García, at
which it would be definitely decided whether the SAINT LOUIS
refugees would be allowed to land and if so, the conditions
under which they would be permitted to stay in Cuban territory. He said that Mr. Clasing had informed him that he had
until tomorrow (i.e. June 6) to make final arrangements.
Berenson asked Clasing if that meant until midnight, June 6,
and Clasing said he supposed so. Berenson is under orders
to attend a meeting this morning, June 6, prepared to make
a final offer and state it before the whole group who would
be working on the matter, i.e., the President, Bernardo
García, Señor Ochotorena, Lopez Castro, and García Montes.
The President's statement in the afternoon Spanish press,
Berenson said, seemed to indicate that a solution had been
found.

Berenson made no reference whatever to the conference
the night before with the Ambassador and did not indicate
whether he had seen the Dominican Consul or had gotten in
touch with Colonel Batista. He asked me to communicate the
information he had given me to the Ambassador, which I did
immediately after Berenson had hung up.

Coert du Bois
American Consul General

811.11-Gen.
CduB/jml
Copy for the Ambassador

78

AMERICAN CONSULATE GENERAL
HABANA, CUBA, JUNE 6, 1939.

MEMORANDUM FOR THE FILES

STRICTLY CONFIDENTIAL

1:30 P.M.   I have just had a talk with Mario Lazo at the
American Club. He wanted to know whether final disposi-
tion had been made of the SAINT LOUIS case. I said that
I had no information subsequent to the President's statement to the press yesterday afternoon, but I took it for
granted that this was an announcement to the Cuban public
that definite arrangements for the landing of these passengers had been concluded. Lazo said that he thought
that if they were permitted to land under any conditions
most serious consequences would follow. He said that
public opinion was organizing strongly against not only
the passengers on the SAINT LOUIS but also against any
refugees who might come on other boats, and that an
anti-Jewish terrorist society had already been formed.
He said that he feared violence. If, as accordingly to
him, it appears that the United States Government was
responsible in any way, either directly or indirectly,
in effecting the landing of these passengers, he felt
that it would undo the work of at least a year in building up friendship with Cuba. He said we apparently had
no idea of the intensity of the public feeling against
these people. He wanted to know what the quota situation
was and whether there was any reasonable prospect of mov-
ing these people on to the United States within the next
few years. I said I did not think there was. Apparently

he

79

he was in a very pessimistic state of mind. He had been talking with Ramos.

Coert du Bois
American Consul General

811.11-General
CduB/jml
Copy for the Ambassador

80

(Enclosure No. 12 to Despatch No. 1017, dated June 7, 1939,
entitled "Jewish Refugee Situation in Habana" --
American Consulate General, Habana, Cuba.

AMERICAN CONSULATE GENERAL
Habana, Cuba, June 6, 1939.

MEMORANDUM FOR THE FILES

STRICTLY CONFIDENTIAL

At 1:30 P. M. today Berenson called me at the American
Club and said he wanted to see me at once. I said I would
be at my office in ten minutes and met him here about 1:45.
He said that the attached proposition for guaranteeing the
support of the passengers on board the SS SAINT LOUIS, providing they were admitted into Cuba, was worked out during
the night and presented to the President by Major Bernardo
García about 4:00 P.M. June 5. It was given by Bustamante
to Major Garcia not later than 2:00 P.M. but did not get to
the President until the time stated. The President's statement to the press stating the terms under which he was willing to consider the admission of the SAINT LOUIS passengers
to Cuba and setting a dead-line of noon, June 6 for negotiations, was released about 3:30 P. M. on June 5, and therefor
before he had had an opportunity to read and consider the
attached proposition. About 1:00 P.M., (June 6) so Berenson tells
me, Ochoterena released to the newspapers a statement that
the President's conditions had not been met, thereby indicating that the attached offer was not satisfactory. At about
1:00 P.M. while Berenson and Bustamante were waiting in the
latter's office for Major Bernardo Garcia to return from
his last interview with the President, Garcia telephoned
from the Palace and told Bustamante to tell Berenson that

81

he

he was leaving immediately to see Colonel Batista and that
he would telephone on his return from Camp Columbia.
Berenson asked for my reaction on what this might mean.
I said his guess was as good as mine but that apprently
it indicated that the meeting at Camp Columbia between
the President, Colonel Batista and Major Garcia did not
come off last night. It struck me that Bernardo Garcia's
visit to Batista which was notified to Berenson from the
Palace might indicate (a) that he was proceeding to Camp
Columbia at the President's request and (b) that the President wanted Batista's backing either in putting an end to
all negotiations and telling the Hamburg-America Line to
take the ship back to Germany or in saving his face should
he recede from his previous position where he demanded a
strict enforcement of the law which required the posting
of a $500 cash bond by each person. It was my opinion,
and I told Berenson to that effect, that his confreres
in New York had better prepare for the worst. I also told
him that in my opinion he and his co-religionists in New
York had gotten this matter off the plane of humanitarianism
and on the plane of horse-trading and if "negotiations"
fail they would be in a position of caring for the plight
of their fellow Jews only for $459,080 _$443,000 worth_ while the President
would be in the position of enforcing the perfectly defined
terms of a law which was known to everybody before these
people left Europe.

Coert du Bois
American Consul General

811.11-
CduB/jml
Copy for the Ambassador

S.S. SAINT LOUIS

Total passengers		933	
Less those under 16 years of age	162		
Less tourists who will go to U.S.	25	187	
		746 at $500 each	$373,000.

S. S. FLANDRE (French)

Total passengers	103	
Less those under 16 years of age	20	
	83 at $500 each	$ 41,500.

S. S. ORDUÑA (English)

83

Total passengers	72	
Less those under 16 years of age	15	
	57 at $500 each	$ 28,500.

Total received from all passengers at $500 each	$443,000.

- - - - - - - - -

How it is proposed to pay this deposit of $443,000.

1. Cash which will be deposited immediately by the Committee in the National City Bank in Habana to be delivered to the Treasury $200,000.

2. Deposits made or to be made to the Treasury:
   a) Cash to be provided immediately by the Committee in Habana   50,000.
   b) Deposited by 16 passengers from SAINT LOUIS   8,000.
   c) Deposited by 50 passengers from FLANDRE   25,000.
   d) Deposited by 14 passengers from ORDUÑA   7,000.

Total in cash	$290,000.

The Committee promises to obtain "with all rapidity" the delivery of the difference,   153,000.

$443,000.

Any excess which is obtained from relatives of the refugees on board these boats, will be delivered to the Secretariat of the Treasury for the amortization of the deposit of $200,000.

(Enclosure No. 13 to Despatch No. 1017, dated June 7, 1939,
entitled "Jewish Refugee Situation in Habana" --
American Consulate General, Habana, Cuba.

AMERICAN CONSULATE GENERAL
Habana, Cuba, June 6, 1939

STRICTLY CONFIDENTIAL

MEMORANDUM FOR THE FILES

At 6:00 P.M. today Berenson telephoned me at my house
and said he had a matter of utmost urgency to discuss with
me at once and could he come and see me immediately. He
arrived 15 minutes later and showed me an English translation of the statement of Oohotorena which was published in
the "Avance" and "Pais" this afternoon, and which indicated
in no uncertain terms that the President's conditions for
the landing of the SAINT LOUIS passengers had not been met
and that the case was closed and the ship was proceeding
to Europe. I sent out a boy and got both papers and found
the statement had in fact been published. Berenson then
proceeded to pronounce a long and rambling discourse which
last until 8:00 P. M., during which I can remember the following disconnected items of some interest:

1. He had never seen Batista.

2. During the visit of Colonel Bonitez to the
Hotel, which Miss Razovsky had described to me as being a
purely formal visit for the purpose of apologizing, more
or less, for his father, Colonel Benitez had made a dis-
tinct bid for $400,000 to $500,000 graft, in addition to
the bond money, to be distributed, among others, between
himself, Pedraza, and a "campaign fund", the last to be
$180,000. The only evidence that such a demand might
possibly be authentic was a note in the President's

handwriting

handwriting that Bustamante had seen (but Berenson had not seen), purporting to direct that all negotiations be made through Major Bernardo García. Since the Major was the open and avowed agent of the President during later legal negotiations, it would seem that this note was not any indication that the President was inviting graft.

3. He said that during the course of the negotiations he had been annoyed by telephone calls from his principals in New York urging him to meet the President's full demands and stating that the money was available. He had replied to these that if they would keep out of it and let him run it he would save them a considerable amount of money.

The remainder of the talk was rambling, incoherent, and often abusive and obscene. This interview was reported to the Ambassador by phone immediately after Berenson had left.

- - - - -

June 7, 1939

At 12:30 P.M. I received a telephone call from Mr. Avra M. Warren, Chief of the Visa Division, Department of State, Washington. Mr. Warren said that leading financiers in New York were instructing the Habana Manager of the Chase National Bank to get in touch with the American Ambassador and ask him to arrange an interview with President Laredo Bru, at which the Manager of the Bank was authorized to offer whatever sums were considered necessary by the President to meet the full conditions of Cuban law and

permit

85

permit the entry of the passengers of the SAINT LOUIS providing that the gate was not entirely closed. He went on to say that under no circumstances and in spite of considerable pressure would he or the Secretary of State or the President give me or the American Ambassador in Habana any instructions to intervene in the matter of the landing of the SAINT LOUIS refugees nor, presumably, of any other European refugees. He said he wanted to make the position of the Department perfectly clear in this matter and repeated these instructions twice, and corroborated me when I repeated them back to him. He said that should the local manager of the Chase National Bank approach the Ambassador with any such request that the Ambassador's action would be left entirely to his own good judgment and whatever he found it wise to do, it was to be understood that he did not do so under instructions from the Secretary of State.

He said he had had several interviews with Secretary Hull and that word had come from the White House, all to this effect. He asked me the status of the situation in Habana and I told him so far as local negotiations were concerned, they appeared to have broken down. I did not know where the ship was nor what its orders were.

I reported the foregoing verbally to the Ambassador at the Embassy at 1:00 P. M.

Coert du Bois
American Consul General

811.11-General
CduB/jml

Copy for the Ambassador

No. 836

STRICTLY CONFIDENTIAL

To the American Ambassador,

London.

The Secretary of State encloses, for the strictly confidential information of the Vice Director of the Intergovernmental Committee on Political Refugees, a copy of despatch no. 1017 from the American Consulate General at Habana, Cuba, dated June 7, 1939, concerning the Jewish refugee situation in Habana.

87

CR ✓

JUN 27 1939 PM

Enclosure:

As stated.

Eu:SM:EMC
6-27-39

Deutsche Gesandtschaft
Havana
(Legación Alemana)

Habana, den 11.Mai 1939.

T.Nr.1022/39

Mit Bezug auf den Bericht vom 1.
Februar ds.Js. - T.Nr.222/39 -

Inhalt: Neue kubanische Einreisebestimmungen.

3 Anlagen.

Auswärtiges Amt
83-216 4/5
eing. 3. MAI 1939
8 Inl. 12/Durchschl.

In der Anlage beehre ich mich ein neues kubanisches
Dekret vom 5.ds.Mts. - No.937 - in einem Ausschnitt aus
der Gaceta Oficial No.284 von gleichem Datum nebst einer
deutschen Uebersetzung vorzulegen.

Das Dekret bringt verschiedene Abänderungen des Dekrets vom 13.Januar ds.Js. und bezieht sich hauptsächlich
auf dessen Artikel II und IV. Es ist am 5.ds.Mts. bereits
in Kraft getreten und bestimmt im im wesentlichen das
Nachstehende:

Alle Touristen nichtamerikanischer Nationalität, die
in Kuba landen wollen, müssen noch vor ihrer Einschiffung
im Besitz der Einreisegenehmigung seitens der Staatssekretäre des Auswärtigen und der Arbeit neben der der
Einwanderungsbehörde sein. Einwanderer müssen ausserdem
einen Garantiebetrag von $ 500.- hinterlegen. Das Dekret
bestimmt ferner, dass die Schiffahrtsgesellschaften den
Staatssekretären des Auswärtigen, der Finanzen und der
Arbeit vollständige Listen der ankommenden und abreisend
Passagiere vorzulegen haben, damit auf diese Weise festgestellt werden kann, ob nicht vielleicht einzelne Pass
giere illegal im Lande geblieben sind. Die Schiffahrts
gesellschaften, die gegen diese Bestimmungen verstosse
haben für alle Kosten des Aufenthalts der Einwanderer
Kuba und ihrer Heimbeförderung aufzukommen.

Die neuen Bestimmungen bringen eine weitere Er-
schwerung der Einreise von Ausländern in Kuba und si
in erster Linie auf die Juden, die in immer grösser
Menge

An das

Auswärtige Amt,

BERLIN.

Mengen häufig schwarz oder gegen Bezahlung von Bestechungsgeldern hier einreisen, gemünzt. Wie ich von gut unterrichteter Seite höre, ist das Dekret zum Teil auch das Ergebnis des Neides der Staatssekretäre des Auswärtigen und der Arbeit auf den Generaldirektor der Einwanderungsbehörde Manuel Benitez y Gonsales, der bereits eine halbe Million Dollar an Bestechungsgeldern eingeheimst hat. Wie dem auch sei, die Einwanderung der Juden wird von jetzt ab in Kuba eingeschränkt werden.

Verschiedene Schiffe, die bereits unterwegs sind, oder vor dem Auslaufen stehen, bringen hierher Passagiere mit nach den früheren Bestimmungen ordnungsmässig erteilten Einreisegenehmigungen. Da solche jedoch nach dem neuen, am 5.ds.Mts. in Kraft getretenen Dekret ihre Gültigkeit verloren haben, würden solche Passagiere am Landen verhindert werden. Angesichts dieses unhaltbaren Zustandes (es sollen mit den Schiffen "Iberia" und "St.Louis" rund 1000 Juden aus Deutschland kommen, deren Heimkehr nicht in unserem Interesse liegen würde) habe ich mich auf Antrag der hiesigen Hapag-Agentur mit der abschriftlich beiliegenden Note an den Staatssekretär Remos gewandt und ihn gebeten, die Passagiere deutscher Schiffe, die nach Habana unterwegs sind und vor dem 5. ds.Mts, die Einreisegenehmigung erhalten haben, ungehindert landen zu lassen. Entsprechende Schritte sind auch vom englischen Gesandten und vom französischen Geschäftsträger unternommen worden. Im übrigen hat der Generaldirektor der Einwanderungsbehörde in einem im beiliegenden Ausschnitt aus dem "Diario de la Marina" veröffentlichten Rundschreiben zur allgemeinen Kenntnis gebracht, dass die auf Grund der früheren Bestimmungen vor dem 6.Mai erteilten Einreisegenehmigungen noch gültig sein würden.

Ueber den weiteren Verlauf der Angelegenheit darf ich mir einen Bericht vorbehalten.

Einige Zeitungsausschnitte betr. das neue Dekret sind in der Anlage beigefügt.

Dekret No.937.

Da durch das Dekret No.55 vom 13.Januar ds.Js.
die Vorschriften für das Landen von Einwanderern in
Cuba festgelegt worden sind, und darin dem Arbeitsminister aus den in den verschiedenen Punkten des erwähnten Dekrets auseinandergesetzten Gründen grösseres
Mitbestimmungsrecht zuerkannt ist,

Da die Praxis die Abänderung einiger der in Kraft
befindlichen Bestimmungen angeraten erscheinen lässt,

bestimme ich, kraft der mir durch die Verfassung
der Republik als Ausführender Gewalt zustehenden Befugnisse und auf den Vorschlag des Staatssekretärs der
Finanzen hin:

ERSTENS: Artikel II des Dekretes No.55 vom 13.Januar
ds.Js. lautet wie folgt:

ARTIKEL II: Ausländern, dören Einwanderung nicht
durch den vorangehenden oder irgend einen anderen Artikel verboten ist, kann die Erlaubnis, in Nationalge-
biet zu landen, erteilt werden, wenn sie einen Garantiebetrag von 500 Pesos hinterlegen.

Diese Erlaubnis muss persönlich von den Staatssekretären des Auswärtigen und der Arbeit gegeben werden.
Sie ist von diesen Beamten direkt und schriftlich den
Schiffahrtsgesellschaften noch vor der Einschiffung
der zur Einreise Ermächtigten im Abfahrtshafen mitzuteilen.

ZWEITENS: Absatz a) des Artikels IV des betreffenden
Dekrets lautet wie folgt:

a) Nur die Turisten, die amerikanische Staatsbürger
sind d.h. diejenigen Personen der genannten Nationalität, die zum Vergnügen reisen und während ihres Aufenthaltes in Lande sich keiner Arbeit widmen. Die Turisten
anderer Nationalität müssen sich nur die Erlaubnis ver-
schaffen, auf die sich der zweite Paragraph des Artikels II bezieht, und haben nicht nötig, einen Garantiebetrag zu hinterlegen.

DRITTENS:

DRITTENS: Der zweite Paragraph des Absatzes c) des
Artikels IV des erwähnten Dekrets hat folgenden
Wortlaut:

Der Kapitän des Schiffs und dessen Konsignatäre
sind verpflichtet, den Hafenbehörden und den Sekretären
des Auswärtigen, der Finanzen und der Arbeit von den
Passagieren Kenntnis zu geben, die nur als Durchreisende
an Land gehen und von denen, die im Lande bleiben.

Die Verkehrsgesellschaften, auf deren Schiffen
die Passagiere reisen, sind verpflichtet, den Hafenbehörden und den Staatssekretären des Auswärtigen, der Finanzen und der Arbeit mitzuteilen, wenn die Durchreisenden
nach Ablauf der 30 Tage, vom Tage der Ankunft in Cuba
an gerechnet, sich nicht wieder eingeschifft haben.

VIERTENS: Artikel IV des verschiedentlich erwähnten
Dekrets No.55 wird durch folgenden Paragraphen er-
weitert:

Die Verkehrsgesellschaften, die Reisende nach
Habana oder anderen Häfen der Republik als Bestimmungs-
hafen bringen, sind verpflichtet, bei Ankunft ihrer
Schiffe den Staatssekretären des Auswärtigen, der Finanzen
und der Arbeit eine ausführliche Aufstellung einzusenden,
in der Name und Herkunft eines jeden Reisenden genau angegeben sind, und beim Verlassen des Hafens eine zweite
Liste vorzulegen, in der die Reisenden aufgeführt sind,
die die Reise fortsetzen. In der Liste sollen auch
diejenigen Reisenden vermerkt sein, die im Lande zurück-
geblieben sind.

FUENFTENS: Artikel V des Dekrets 2507 vom 17.November
1938, der in der Gaceta Oficial vom 25. des gleichen
Monats veröffentlicht ist, lautet wie folgt:

ARTIKEL V: Die diplomatischen und konsularischen
Behörden der Republik haben über alle Fälle zu berichten, in denen Ausländer beabsichtigen, nach Cuba zu gehen
und den Garantiebetrag zu hinterlegen sowie die Landungserlaubnis in Uebereinstimmung mit den Einwanderungsvor-
schriften einzuholen haben. Sie haben ferner den Beruf,
den die in Frage stehenden Ausländer ausüben, anzugeben.

In

91

In solchen Fällen brauchen sie nur die Sichtvermerke auszustellen, vorausgesetzt, dass sie dazu die vorherige Ermächtigung seitens des Aussen- und Arbeitsministeriums im Benehmen mit dem Finanzministerium erhalten haben, Vorbedingungen, ohne die die Sichtvermerke ungültig sind.

Erforderlich ist die Erteilung eines Einreisesichtvermerks für Ausländer, die nicht nordamerikanische Bürger sind, sich nach Cuba begeben und unter die Abschnitte d) und e) des Artikels IV des Dekrets No.55 vom Jahre 1939 fallen. Um den Sichtvermerk in diesen Fällen erteilen zu können, ist es erforderlich, dass der diplomatische oder konsularische Beamte hierzu durch den Staatssekretär des Auswärtigen ermächtigt wird, nachdem die Einreise solcher Ausländer nach Cuba durch den Staatssekretär der Finanzen im Benehmen mit dem Staatssekretär für Erziehung bewilligt worden ist.

92

SECHSTENS: Die Verkehrsgesellschaften, die Ausländer nach Cuba bringen, die unter die Einwanderungsgesetze fallen und die darin vorgesehenen Bestimmungen nicht erfüllt haben, sind verantwortlich für die Kosten, die durch solche Verstösse verursacht werden, und zwar für die Kosten während ihres Aufenthaltes in Cuba sowie für die der Rückverschiffung. Sie werden hierfür entweder vom Finanzministerium auf administrativem Wege der Zwangsvollstreckung, durch Einleitung eines dienstlichen Gerichtsverfahrens oder auf dem Klagewege durch das Aussen- oder Handelsministerium zur Verantwortung gezogen.

In gleicher Weise werden die Verkehrsgesellschaften verantwortlich gemacht für Durchreisende, die im Lande bleiben, desgleichen die Unternehmen, welche die Passagen von Cuba bis zum Bestimmungsorte im Auslande für solche Durchreisende ausgestellt haben, die innerhalb der 30 Tage, vom Tage der Ankunft in Cuba an gerechnet, nicht nach ihren Bestimmungsorte weitergereist sind.

SIEBENTENS: Die Staatssekretäre des Auswärtigen, der Finanzen und der Arbeit haben dafür Sorge zu tragen, dass das Dekret in den sie betreffenden Teilen richtig durchgeführt

geführt wird.

ACHTENS: Alle Dekrete, Verordnungen, Beschlüssen und
Bestimmungen, die der Ausführung der Bestimmungen des
vorliegenden Dekrets entgegen sind, werden hiermit
aufgehoben. Das Dekret tritt mit dem Tage seiner Veröffentlichung in der Gaceta Oficial der Republik in
Kraft.

    Gegeben im Präsidentenpalast in Habana, am
5.Mai 1939

                    ges. Federico Laredo
                      Präsident

ges. Oscar Garcia Montes
    Finanzsekretär.

Telegramm (geh.Ch.V.)

Havana, den 2.Juni 1939   O Uhr 04

Ankunft: 2. "   "   8 " ?5

Nr.35 vom 1/6.   Bezug Bericht vom 11.Mai T 1022.

Die Kubanische Regierung hat,nachdem wiederholte Schritte
der Gesandtschaft erfolglos geblieben,heute um 15 Uhr Hapag-
Agenten Wortlaut heutigen,noch nicht veröffentlichten Dekrets
des Staatspräsidenten durch Zollchef aushändigen lassen,in
dem Verlassen Hafens durch Schiff »San Luis« ,das seit 27.
April mit über 900 jüdischen Emigranten hier liegt, mit Besatzung und Passagieren noch am heutigen Tag verlangt wird.
Begründung hierfür neben Nichtbeachtung Einwanderungsbestimmungen durch Schiffsgesellschaft und Passagiere Gefährdung
der öffentlichen Ordnung durch Unruhe unter den Passagieren.
Andernfalls würde Schiff durch Kriegsmarine ausserhalb
Hoheitsgewässer gebracht werden. Besatzungsmitglieder, die
illegal an Land sind,würden durch die Polizei an
Bord gebracht werden.

    Inzwischen Frist Aufenthalts bis morgen 18 Uhr
zwecks Verproviantierung verlängert.

    Einlege sofort Protest gegen ungebührliche Be-
handlung Schiffes und Gewaltandrohung.

    Schriftbericht folgt.

    Telegramm hat Hoheitsträger vorgelegen.

                                    Kaempfe

94

Nr. 154.
USA.   5. Juni 1939.   Blatt - 3
                                                   nittags

N e w   Y o r k, 5.Juni. Morgenblätter berichten grossaufgemacht
über Führer-Rede Kassel. Berlindepesche Nytimeskorrespondeten c
Enderis bemerkt Kriegertagung sicherlich demonstrativste sympa-
thischste Zuhörerschaft, die Hitler jemals gegenüberstand. Er
sprach als Soldat zu Soldaten aber Rede war erneutes Friedensbe-
kenntnis. Bemerkung betreffs Absetzung irgendeiner Person die
nicht hundertprozent Mann Soldat, werde bestimmt Neugierde erregen
angesichts kürzlicher unbestätigter Meldungen weiterer Verschiebun-
gen der Armee. Assopress bringt Redetext mit Bemerkung sei Übersetzung Hit-
lerrede wie vom DNB kondensiert und ausgegeben.

N e w   Y o r k, 5.Juni. Assopress berichtet aus Miami Florida
Hapagdampfer St. Louis mit 907 Juden aus Deutschland an Bord, der
anscheinend ziellos herumfahre, um Ergebnis Bemühungen abzuwarten, Landungserlaubnis Kubas zu erwirken ankerte zweistündig drei
Meilen weit von Miamibeach. Zwei Küstenwachflugzeuge wurden zwecks
Überwachung Dampfers entsandt. Nach zwei Stunden fortsetzte St.
Louis-Fahrt südöstlich. Assopress Havanna New Yorker Anwalt Berenson konferierte mit Präsidenten Bru anderen Regierungsbeamten betreffs Zulassung Juden, ablehnte anzugeben, ob Bemühungen erfolg-
reich. Washington Amtskreise erwägen Assopress zufolge Möglichkeit Ansiedlung zehntausender Juden aus Deutschland in Philippinen,
um Einfluss dortiger Japaner entgegenzuwirken. Entscheidung erfolge
erst nach Rückkehr des kürzlich nach Philippinen zur Prüfung Frage
entsandten Sonderausschusses.

          Nyheraldtribune bringt Londonartikel erklärend,
Zusammenhalten Polens Griechenlands Rumäniens Türkei Sowjetruss-
lands Englands darstelle neuen Völkerbund der sicheren Grundlage
Selbstinteresses gebildet werde.
W a s h i n g t o n, 5. Juni. - Auf hier abgehaltenen nationalen
Versammlung sogenannter Oxfordgruppe für moralische Wiederauf-
rüstung verlas Bundessenator Truman folgende Botschafter Roosevelts
zugrundeliegende Kraft der Welt muss in moralischer Natur ihrer
Bürger bestehen. Ein Programm moralischer Wiederaufrüstung der Welt...

                    83-26 (Kuba)

Nr. 156.   m o r g e n s

U S A.   Von 7. Juni 1939 .   Blatt - 5 -
-.-

N e w   Y o r k, 6. Juni.- Scotland Yard und die USA-Geheimpolizei
leiteten der New Yorker Stadtverwaltung und Polizei folgende Verhal-
tungsmassregeln für die New Yorker Bürgerschaft zu, die während des
britischen Königsbesuchs in New York-Stadt und auf der Weltausstellung
am nächsten Samstag genau zu befolgen seien: 1.) Beim Vorbeifahren der
Majestäten muss jeder Zuschauer stillstehen und jegliche Bewegung unter-
lassen, 2.) jedes Fenster in jedem Gebäude entlang der Strassen, durch
die das Königspaar fährt, muss geschlossen bleiben, 3.) die Polizei muss
auf den Dächern der Wolkenkratzer und anderer hoher Gebäude aufgestellt
sein, von wo die Menge überwacht werden kann, 4.) die Polizei muss an
allen Pfeilern unter der 8 km langen Auto-Hochbahn postiert sein,
über die das Königspaar führt sowie vor allen Gebäuden, Hauseingängen,
Strassenecken entlang der Fahrtroute. "World Telegram" bemerkt hierzu
die Instruktionen besagten nicht, was die New Yorker Polizei tun solle,
wenn es sich die Zuschauer einfallen liessen dem Königspaar zuzuwinken,
ob die Polizei ihn dann sofort fesseln und verhaften oder erst durch
einen Schlag mit dem Gummiknüppel harmlos machen solle. Auch sei uner-
wähnt, wieviele Maschinengewehre auf den Dächern der Wolkenkratzer
erwünscht sind.

            Aus Havana (Kuba).- Der Präsident gab bekannt, dass die
kubanische Regierung den 907 jüdischen Emigranten an Bord der "St.Louis"
nunmehr endgültig die Landungserlaubnis entzogen habe, nachdem die
amerikanisch-jüdischen Organisationen, die versprachen die erforderliche
Kaution von 500 Dollars pro Kopf zu stellen, den von der Regierung
Kubas festgesetzten letzten Termin, Dienstag Mittag 12 Uhr, nicht ein-
hielten.

            Lt. Mitteilung des New Yorker Büros der Hapag-Lloyd befindet
sich die "St. Louis" bereits seit Montag auf dem Rückweg nach Hamburg.

96

Eigentum des Deutschen Nachrichtenbüros (DNB)

Geheimmittel — Nur zur streng persönlichen Unterrichtung des Empfängers.

(Ohne redaktionelle Verantwortung.)

Nr. 160   abends

A n g l o   11.Juni 1939   Blatt 8
- -

..verschmolzen worden ist, der seit 1 1/2 Jahren Lord Kemsley unter-
steht. Das jüdische Blatt, das führend in der Deutschenhetze war,
wird jetzt auch bereits auf der Linken und in den Reihen der Hetzer
schmerzlich vermisst. Der stark deutschfeindlich eingestellte "Sunday
Dispatch" erklärt, das Verschwinden des "Sunday Refery" sei ein Schock
und tief zu bedauern. Das Blatt hat denn auch sofort sich Artikel der
Madame Tabouis gesichert, die mit dem Verschwinden des "Sunday Refery"
ihre publizistische Basis in London verloren hatte. Der "Sunday Dispatch"glaubt daher, seine Spalten der Dame zur Verfügung stellen zu
müssen. Der stark kommunistische eingestellte "Reynolds News" lamen-
tiert am meisten und erklärt, dass nunmehr "Reynaulds News" sich be-
rufen fühle, die "unabhängige" Linie des "Sunday Refery" fortzusetzen.
Der "Sunday Refery" hat bekanntlich Isidor Osterer gehört, der zusammen mit seinen Brüdern den führenden englischen Filmkonzern, die
"British Gaumont" kontrolliert und die daher im Volksmund die "Jiddi-
sche Gaumont" heisst. Auch dieser Filmkonzern benutzt bekanntlich sein
Macht zur übelsten Deutschenhetze.

L o n d o n , 11. Juni. WieReuter berichtet, haben die 907 Juden an
Bord des Hapag-Dampfers "St. Louis", die bekanntlich vergeblich in
Kuba zu landen versuchten, telegraphisch Chamberlain um die Erlaubnis
ersucht, in Southampton landen zu dürfen. In dem Telegramm haben sie
erklärt, es sei ihnen unmöglich, nach Hamburg zurückzukehren und sie
befänden sich daher in verzweifelter Lage.

L o n d o n, 11. Juni. Die Sonntagspresse beachtet weiter die Vorgänge in Kladno im Protektorat Böhmen und Mähren stark, gibt aber die
letzten Nachrichten neutral und in sichtlich ruhiger Form wieder.

97

HAMBURG-AMERIKA LINIE

HENNING VON MEIBOM
Direktor und Repräsentant

BERLIN W 8, den
Unter den Linden 61

116781

An das
Auswärtige Amt
z.Hd. von Herrn Geheimrat Freytag
B e r l i n W.8
Wilhelmstr. 74-76

Sehr geehrter Herr Geheimrat !

Wir haben am 13.Mai von Hamburg abgehend
unser MS. "St. Louis" nach Havanna expediert, das ca. 930
nahezu ausnahmslos jüdische Emigranten an Bord hatte, und das
am 27.Mai in Havanna angekommen ist. Unsere Vertretung hat
sich in der Zwischenzeit bemüht - also ca. eine Woche - die
Landung dieser ca. 930 Passagiere durchzuführen.

Wir erhalten nun heute früh folgendes Kabel
von unserer Vertretung in Havanna, das für sich selbst spricht:

"ms. st.louis received order by decree of president to leave
harbour. forthwith opposition would involve action of war
marine. german legation informed. expected to sail on friday at 10.00 a.m. is there any possibility and where to
land passengers other than germany ? telegraph immediately
in order to complete set of charts for eventuality."

Fernerhin erhalten wir aus New York ein
Kabel, in dem unsere Vertretung uns folgendes mitteilt :

"ms. st.louis havana resulting wide spread publicity in
this country mentioning suicide state of mutiny among the
passengers thus stirring quite some feeling. our opinion
is ship should remain havana as long as slight possibility
landing of passengers there or neighbouring country. 1st
cruise must be cancelled probably and although this may
influence later cruises to such an extent that these must
be withdrawn we prefer this risk to facing further unfa-
vourable publicity account hurried departure from havana."

Zu diesem letzteren Teil dieses Kabels
beginnend mit "1st cruise" möchte ich bemerken, daß wir beabsichtigt haben, das Schiff nach Rückkehr von der Havana-
reise in Ballast nach New York zu schicken, um von dort aus
Westindien-Vergnügungsreisen zu unternehmen. Wir beabsichtigten in erster Linie hiermit, möglichst viele Devisen auf die-

83 26

- 2 -

Drahtwort: Hapag Berlin / Fernruf: Sammelnummer 116781

98

sen Reisen Reisen einzufahren.

      Ich werde mir erlauben, Sie heute nachmittag
, nachdem Sie diesen Brief zur Kenntnis genommen haben,
gegen 5 Uhr anzurufen.

          Mit verbindlichsten Empfehlungen und
             Heil Hitler !
          Ihr sehr ergebener

<u>Abschrift Kult.K 646</u>

Deutsche Gesandtschaft   Habana, den 1.Februar 1939.
   T.Nr. 222/39

Mit Bezug auf Bericht vom 28.11.1938
T.Nr. 1924/38-

Inhalt: Kubanische Einreisebestimmungen. ·

1 Anlage

      In der Anlage lege ich ein neues kubanisches Dekret
No.55 vom 13.Januar 1939, abgedruckt in der "Gaceta oficial" No.
34 vom 16.Januar 1939 vor.

      Das Dekret faßt die bisher bestehenden grundsätzlichen
Bestimmungen des Dekretes No.1021 vom 23.März 1937 (eingereicht mit
Berichten vom 3.April 1937 -K.Nr.60- und vom 25.April 1938 -T.Nr.
571/38-) und des Dekretes No.2507 vom 17.November 1938 (eingereicht
mitdem oben angezogenen Bericht) zusammen und bestimmt:

100

    1.) Grundsätzlich sind alle Personen, die der öffentlichen
        Fürsorge zur Last fallen können, von der Zulassung in
        Kuba ausgeschlossen.

    2.) Die einreisenden Ausländer müssen einen Sicherheitsbetrag
        von Pesos 500.- hinterlegen.

      Hierzu darf bemerkt werden, daß in letzter Zeit eine
große Anzahl deutscher Juden unter Beihilfe von Agenten des jüdischen Hilfskomitees und Einwanderungsbeamten schwarz oder gegen Bezahlung eines Bestechungsgeldes, das in die Taschen der Einwanderungsbeamten geflossen ist, eingereist sind.

    3.) Der Sicherheitsbetrag soll in bar gezahlt werden

    4.) Ohne Hinterlegung werden zugelassen:
        a) Touristen, die zum Vergnügen reisen und in Kuba keine
           Arbeit nehmen,
        b) Transitpassagiere während des Aufenthaltes ihres
           Dampfers im Hafen,
        c) durchreisende Passagiere, die im Besitz ihrer Passage
           sind und sich nicht länger als 30 Tage hier aufhalten,
        d) Konferenzteilnehmer, Künstler, Wissenschaftler, sofern
           sie keine andere Erwerbstätigkeit in Kuba ausüben,
        e) Geistliche.
                      Infolge

Infolge Gegenseitigkeit sind alle Staatsbürger der Vereinigten Staaten von dem Hinterlegungszwang befreit.

Die Ausländer der Gruppen a) bis d) müssen unter Eid einen Fragebogen ausfüllen.

5.) Kein Kubaner gilt als Tourist

6.) Art.5 des Dekretes Nr.2507 vom 15. November 1938 wird dahin geändert, daß die kubanischen Missionen und Konsulate im Ausland über alle Personen, die unter Ziffer 2 fallen, unter Angabe ihres Berufes berichten und die Sichtvermerkserteilung von der Weisung des kubanischen Außenministeriums abhängig machen sollen.

7.) Die Einwanderungsbehörde soll innerhalb 48 Stunden dem Arbeitsminister alle Personalangaben über jeden eingereisten Ausländer machen. Das Gleiche gilt für die Ausreise von Ausländern.

8.) Zugelassene Ausländer, die länger als 6 Monate von Kuba abwesend sind, verlieren ihr Recht auf Niederlassung.

9.) Die hinterlegten Sicherheitsbeträge sollen auf Postsparkonto eingezahlt werden.

10.) Der hinterlegte Betrag von Pesos 500.- soll auf Antrag nach zwei Jahren zurückgezahlt werden, wenn der Antragsteller nicht der öffentlichen Fürsorge anheimgefallen ist. Vor Ablauf von zwei Jahren wird der Betrag im Falle der Ausreise zurückgegeben.

11.) Die Tatsache der Befreiung von der Hinterlegung berechtigt nicht zur Befreiung von dem Sichervermerkszwang.

12/13.) Chinesen sollen grundsätzlich nicht einreisen.

14.) Außen-, Finanz-, Erziehungs- und Arbeitsministerium, sowie die Verwaltung der Postsparkasse werden mit Ausführung des Dekrets beauftragt.

15.) Das Dekret No.1021 vom 23.März 1937, mit Ausnahme seines Artikels 6, und die übrigen hiedurch überholten Dekrete und Bestimmungen werden aufgehoben.

gez. Völckers.

An das Auswärtige Amt, Berlin.

Deutsche Gesandtschaft
Havana
(Legación Alemana)

T.Nr.1111/39

Inhalt: Wachsender Antisemitismus in Cuba.

8 Anlagen.

Habana, den 25.Mai 1939.

In letzter Zeit macht sich in einem grösseren Teil der hiesigen Presse ein Erstarken der antijüdischen Campagne bemerkbar. Es handelt sich hier vor allem um die Zeitungen "Diario de la Marina", "Avance" und das im Verlage des "Diario de la Marina" erscheinende Mittagsblatt "Alerta". Das Letztere brachte eine Reihe von Artikeln, in denen es heisst, dass die Juden in den hiesigen Handel eindringen, die Cubaner in rücksichtsloser Weise ausbeuten, ja auch aus dem Handel herauszudrängen beginnen, ferner dass sie die Gesetze des Landes verletzen bezw. umgehen und die cubanischen Behörden betrügen. Die Zeitung verlangt, dass die cubanische Regierung die Juden als unerwünschte und lästige Elemente schleunigst ausweist, und bezeichnet sie als Polypen, die dem cubanischen Volkskörper das Blut aussaugen. Einer von den genannten Artikeln trägt die unmissverständliche Ueberschrift "Hinaus mit den Juden".

In einem "La amenaza inmigratoria" überschriebenen Artikel des Abendblattes "Avance" werden die Gefahren eines weiteren Eindringens der Juden in Cuba vor Augen geführt. Die Juden, sagt der Artikelschreiber, werden bald den Handel in Cuba beherrschen, und das cubanische Volk wird unter Kapitalisten neuer Prägung, die eine andere Sprache sprechen, an einen anderen Gott glauben und sich nicht um die Sorgen des Landes kümmern, leiden müssen. Interessant ist schliesslich ein Aufsatz der bedeutendsten hiesigen Zeitung "Diario de la Marina", der von dem Inhaber des Blattes, Herrn Dr. José I.Rivero, unter dem Titel "Impresiones" veröffentlicht worden ist. Herr Rivero verlangt hier ausserordentliche Massnahmen gegen die jüdische Einwanderung, damit Situationen, wie im Jahre 1933 (Revolution gegen Machado) vermieden werden.

An das

Auswärtige Amt,

BERLIN.

werden. Die in Frage stehenden Aufsätze sind in der
Anlage beigefügt, desgleichen 2 sehr farblose Artikel
der hiesigen Linkspresse ("Hoy" vom 18.ds.Mts. und "El
Mundo" vom 18.ds.Mts.), die für die Juden eine Lanse
brechen.

Aber nicht in der Presse allein wird jetzt gegen
die jüdische Einwanderung Front gemacht. Auch in Re-
gierungs- und Parlamentskreisen ist der Antisemitismus
erwacht. So hat beispielsweise der Vorsitzende des Einwanderungsausschusses der Deputiertenkammer, Pedro Mendieta, den Präsidenten der Republik unter Hinweis darauf,
dass die Juden illegal in Cuba einwandern und cubanischen
Arbeitern das Brot wegnehmen, gebeten, die Landung der
Juden hier gesetzlich zu verbieten. In gleichem Zusammenhang darf ich auch auf das neue Einwanderungsgesetz
vom 5.Mai (vgl.Bericht vom 11.Mai ds.Js. - T.Nr.1022/39 -)
hinweisen, das die Einreise der Juden stark erschwert.

Es ist eine unbestreitbare Tatsache, dass die Juden
dort, wo sie in grösseren Massen sind, sich sehr bald
unbeliebt machen und durch ihr abstossendes Wesen und
unlauteres Handeln den Antisemitismus selbst erzeugen.
In Cuba, wo rund 7 000 Juden eingewandert sind, wird
diese Strömung im Volke wie in Regierungskreisen immer
stärker. Sorgen macht der cubanischen Regierung, wie
mir der Unterstaatssekretär Dr.Campa sagte, vor allem der
Gedanke, dass die Juden, die sich in Cuba in der Regel
als "Durchreisende" oder "Touristen" aufhalten, um später nach den Vereinigten Staaten zu gehen, sich hier definitiv niederlassen könnten.

In Erkennung der grossen jüdischen Gefahr für das
Land wird nach den letzten Zeitungnachrichten demnächst
ein neues Dekret erlassen werden, das die Bestimmungen des
Einwanderungsdekrets vom 5.Mai ds.Js. - No.937 - noch
verschärfen wird und verhindern soll, dass Juden in Cuba
einwandern und cubanische Arbeiter aus ihren Stellen
verdrängen.

Weitere Berichterstattung behalte ich mir ergebenst
vor.

103

Deutsche Gesandtschaft
Havana
(Legación Alemana)

Habana, den 2.Juni 1939.

T.Nr.1143/39

Im Anschluss an den Bericht vom
11.v.Mts. - T.Nr.1022/39 - und an
den anderweitigen Bericht vom
gestern - No.35 - <<

83 - 26 4/6

Inhalt: Hapag-Schiff "San Luis" und Lan-
dungsverbot für jüdische Emigranten in Cuba.

8 Anlagen. (some 29 Zeitungsausschnitte)

104

Am 27.v.Mts. traf um 4 Uhr a.m. im hiesigen Hafen
der Hapag-Dampfer "San Luis" mit 936 jüdischen Emigranten ein. Die Passagiere befanden sich nur zum ganz
geringen Teil im Besitz von cubanischen Einreisesicht-
vermerken, alle übrigen besassen dagegen vor dem 6.Mai
ds.Js. ausgestellte Einreisegenehmigungen des Generaldirektors der hiesigen Einwanderungsbehörde.

Während die cubanischen Behörden die Passagiere
(jüdische Emigranten) des am 15.v.Mts. hier eingetroffe-
nen Dampfers "Iberia" mit der Begründung landen liessen,
dass sie bei Erlass des Einwanderungsdekrets vom 5.v.Mts.
(vgl.Bericht vom 11.Mai ds.Js. - T.Nr.1022/39 -) bereits unterwegs waren, stellten sie sich diesmal auf
den Standpunkt, dass sowohl die Passagiere als auch die
Hapag-Agentur den neuen gesetzlichen Bestimmungen nicht
entsprochen hätten, und untersagten die Landung. Später
wurde allerdings denjenigen Juden, die ein cubanisches
Visum hatten, die Landung gestattet. Das Ausschiffungs-
verbot der überwiegenden Mehrzahl der Juden wurde indessen bis zum Schluss aufrechterhalten, obwohl der
Chef der Einwanderungsbehörde, Oberst Benitez, in seinem abschriftlich beiliegenden offiziellen Schreiben
an die Hapag-Agentur vom 9.v.Mts. ausdrücklich erklärt
hat, dass die von ihm vor dem 6.v.Mts. ausgestellten
Einreisegenehmigungen

das
Auswärtige Amt,

B E R L I N .

Einreisegenehmigungen gültig seien.

Da ich schon bei Veröffentlichung des neuen Einwanderungsdekrets vom 5.v.Mts. voraussah, dass die
Cubaner der Landung der Juden Schwierigkeiten in den
Weg legen würden, ich mir andererseits aber darüber
im Klaren war, dass ihre Rückkehr nach Deutschland
unerwünscht wäre, habe ich mich am 10.v.Mts. mit der
meinem Bericht vom 11.v.Mts. - T.Nr.1022/39 - abschriftlich beigefügten Note an den Staatssekretär Remos gewandt und, da ich keine Antwort erhielt, ihn erneut in
der abschriftlich beiliegenden Note vom 23.v.Mts. gebeten, die Passagiere des Schiffs "San Luis" landen zu
lassen. Eine schriftliche Antwort erhielt ich vom
Staatssekretär auch jetzt nicht. Dagegen erschien bei
mir am Tage des Eintreffens der "San Luis" gegen 10
Uhr a.m. ein Beamter des Protokolls und erklärte mir,
dass der Präsident der Republik die Landung verboten
hätte, da die Bestimmungen des Dekrets vom 5.v.Mts.
von den Passagieren und von der Hapag verletzt worden
seien. Auch zeigte er mir einen Bericht des cubanischen Generalkonsuls in Hamburg, wonach kein einziger
Passagier der "San Luis" eine gültige Einreisegenehmigung für Cuba erhalten hätte. Ich suchte daraufhin
noch am selben Abend in Begleitung eines Herrn der
hiesigen Hapag-Agentur den Staatssekretär Remos auf,
um von ihm wenigstens die Genehmigung zur Freimachung
von Plätzen für etwa 300 Passagiere, die mit der "San
Luis" nach Deutschland reisen sollten, zu erhalten.
Ich bat ihn, die entsprechende Anzahl von Juden landen und zunächst nach dem hiesigen Einwandererlager
Tiscornia bringen zu lassen, wobei die Hapag die Garan-
tie dafür übernehmen würde, dass diese Personen, falls
ihr Verbleiben definitiv abgelehnt werden sollte, in
spätestens sechs bis sieben Wochen Cuba wieder verlassen
würden. Dr.Remos versprach,noch am nächsten Morgen mit
dem Präsidenten der Republik zu sprechen. Der Erfolg
blieb jedoch auch diesmal aus.

Während bis zum gestrigen Tage hier allgemein die
Auffassung

105

Auffassung herrschte, dass die Cubanische Regierung
doch noch die Landungsgenehmigung erteilen würde,
überreichte gestern der hiesige Zollchef Dr.Varona
dem Hapag-Agenten das in dem anderweitigen Bericht
von gestern - No.35 - genannte Dekret des Staatspräsidenten neben einem von ihm unterzeichneten
Begleitschreiben. Beide liegen in der Anlage abschriftlich und in deutscher Uebersetzung bei. Hierin
wurde verlangt, dass der Dampfer "San Luis" noch am
gleichen Tag Habana verlässt, andernfalls er durch
die cubanische Kriegsmarine ausserhalb der Hoheitsgewässer gebracht werden würde. Als Grund hierfür
wurde neben der Nichtbefolgung der Einwanderungsbestimmungen die Gefährdung der öffentlichen Sicherheit (!)
angegeben. Angesichts der unerhörten Behandlung eines
deutschen Schiffs, vor allem aber der Gewaltandrohung
und zu kurzen Fristsetzung für die Verproviantierung
habe ich mich veranlasst gesehen, die abschriftlich
in deutscher und spanischer Sprache in der Anlage beigefügte Note an den Staatssekretär zu richten, worin
ich auch meinen Standpunkt zu den Ausführungen des
Schreibens des Generaldirektors der Einwanderungsbehörde und zur Frage der Gültigkeit der Einwanderungs-
genehmigunen vertrat. Das Schiff "San Luis" hat inzwischen heute vormittag um 11 Uhr 30 Habana in voll-
ster Ruhe und Ordnung verlassen.

Dass die Cubanische Regierung keine Lust ver-
spürt, die zahlreichen jüdischen Emigranten aufzunehmen, ist durchaus verständlich. Auch in Argentinien
und Uruguay ist in den letzten Tagen die Landung von
Juden aus Deutschland nicht gestattet worden. [Es wäre
kaum etwas einzuwenden gewesen, wenn die hiesige Regierung ohne Gewaltandrohung das von den Juden vollbesetzte Schiff veranlasst hätte, den Hafen in angemessener Zeit zu verlassen. Die Art, wie die Regierung
ein deutsches Schiff zu behandeln gewagt hat, hat indessen mit Juden nichts mehr zu tun und stellt eine

Beleidigung

Beleidigung Deutschlands dar, die wir von Cuba, das
schon wiederholt seine anti-deutsche Einstellung
offenbart hat, nicht stillschweigend hinnehmen können.]

Selbstverständlich hat der Aufenthalt der "San
Luis" im Hafen von Habana wieder eine antideutsche
Pressecampagne ausgelöst. Eine Reihe von dreisten und
dummen Hetzartikeln der hiesigen Linkszeitungen "Hoy",
"El Pais" und "El Mundo" und des antideutschen amerikanischen Blatts "Havana Post" füge ich in der Anlage bei.
Andererseits waren auch häufig in der cubanischen Presse antijüdische Aeusserungen zu lesen. Vor allem soll
aber demnächst, verursacht durch den Aufenthalt der
"San Luis" mit rund tausend Juden im hiesigen Hafen,
ein neues Dekret erlassen werden, in dem der Einwanderung der Juden ein Riegel vorgeschoben wird. Ein star-
ker Gegner der jüdischen Einwanderung in Cuba ist der
Vorsitzende des Einwanderungsausschusses der Kammer,
Herr Mendieta, mit dem ich über die Judenfrage eingehend
zu sprechen Gelegenheit hatte. Eine Anzahl von Zeitungsausschnitten betr."San Luis" und das Judenproblem liegt
gleichfalls bei.

Von besonderem Interesse ist der Umstand, dass
eine Reihe von jüdischen Verbänden und Organisationen,
insbesondere aber das Jüdische Hilfskomitee, sich mit
der hiesigen Regierung in Verbindung gesetzt und über
die Frage der Genehmigung der Landung der Juden verhandelt hat und trotz der Abfahrt des Schiffs immer noch
weiter verhandelt. Allein 5 amerikanisch-jüdische An-
wälte, unter ihnen Dr.Lawrence Berenson, Vorsitzender
der Cubanischen Handelskammer in den Vereinigten Staaten und Anwalt des Jüdischen Hilfskomitees für Flüchtlinge, waren hierher gekommen. Wie mir der Hapag-Agent
heute sagte, ist es durchaus wahrscheinlich, dass der
Dampfer "San Luis" noch zurückkehren wird, und dass
die Juden die Landungsgenehmigung schliesslich doch
erhalten werden, da die amerikanisch-jüdischen Organisationen einen sehr beträchtlichen Geldbetrag den Cubanern
hierfür

107

hierfür zu zahlen bereit sein sollen. Auch geht
hier das Gerücht um, dass die Regierung der Domi-
nikanischen Republik den Juden von "San Luis" die
Zuwanderung in Santo Domingo gestattet hätte. Die
nächste Zukunft wird über das Los dieser jüdischen
Emigranten entscheiden.

Für eine baldgefällige Weisung, ob bzw. welche
weiteren Schritte ich wegen der unerhörten Behandlung eines deutschen Schiffs durch die Cubanische
Regierung unternehmen soll, wäre ich dankbar.

NS. Die soeben erhaltene Gaceta Oficial vom 1.
    Juni ds.Js. - No.357 - ist gleichfalls
    beigefügt.

108

Deutsche Gesandtschaft
Habana

Habana, den 1.Juni 1939.

T.Nr.1141/39

Herr Staatssekretär,

In der Anlage beehre ich mich Eurer Exzellenz Abschrift des heute um 3 Uhr p.m. dem Hapag-Agenten übergebenen, wie ich festgestellt habe, bisher noch <u>nicht</u> veröffentlichten, also auch noch nicht in Kraft getretenen Dekrets vom heutigen Datum No. 1168 zu übersenden, wonach das deutsche Schiff "San Luis" noch am heutigen Tage den Hafen von Habana mit Besatzung und Passagieren zu verlassen hat. Für den Fall, dass das Schiff die Anordnung des Dekrets, noch heute den Hafen zu verlassen, nicht erfüllt haben sollte, heisst es in dem Dekret weiter, wird die kubanische Kriegsmarine aufgefordert werden, das Schiff ausserhalb der Hoheitsgewässer zu geleiten. Auch wird hierin bemerkt, dass Besatzungsmitglieder, die "illegal" an Land gegangen sind, durch die Polizei wieder an Bord des Schiffs geschafft werden würden.

Ich muss hierbei darauf hinweisen, dass ein <u>illegales</u> Anlandgehen von Mitgliedern der Besatzungen deutscher Schiffe überhaupt nicht möglich ist, da jedes von Bord gehende Besatzungsmitglied gemeinsam von einem Offizier des Schiffes und der wachhabenden kubanischen Beamten kontrolliert wird.

Ich habe selbstverständlich meine Regierung über die Angelegenheit sofort informiert und erwarte ihre Weisung, bedaure aber jetzt schon das Nachstehende sagen zu müssen:

Nachdem die Gesandtschaft sich an Eure Exzellenz mit den Noten vom 10. und vom 23. v. Mts. - T.Nr. 1006/39 und 1100/39 - in der Angelegenheit der Landung der Passagiere

An Seine Exzellenz
Herrn Dr.Juan J. R e m o s
Staatssekretär des Auswärtigen
H a b a n a

giere deutscher Schiffe gewandt hat, hat sie er-
warten dürfen, dass sie mit einer offiziellen
__schriftlichen__ und begründeten Antwort beehrt werden
würde. Dies ist leider nicht erfolgt. Ferner ist
die Gesandtschaft über das infrage stehende Dekret,
in dem ein deutsches Schiff die Weisung erhält, den
Hafen unter Androhung von Gewalt noch am selben Tage
zu verlassen, durch die Sekretaria de Estado überhaupt nicht unterrichtet worden. Die Gesandtschaft
musste erst von dem Agenten der Hamburg-Amerika
Linie von der aussergewöhnlichen Massnahme, vor allem
aber von der Gewaltandrohung einem deutschen Schiff,
also einem Schiff gegenüber, das unter der Flagge einer befreundeten Nation fährt, in Kenntnis gesetzt
werden. Dass hierbei in dem betreffenden Dekret neben der Gewaltandrohung eine viel zu knappe Zeit für
die Verproviantierung des vollbesetzten Schiffs ge-
währt wurde, ist überhaupt unverständlich. Wenn auch
nachträglich die Frist des Auslaufens bis morgen 6 Uhr
p.m. verlängert worden ist, so bleiben die Tatsache
der zu kurzen Fristsetzung __durch das Dekret__ und die
Gewaltandrohung bestehen. Es ist wohl richtig, dass
das Schiff bereits seit dem 27. v.Mts. hier liegt,
doch darf nicht ausser acht gelassen werden, dass die
Verhandlungen der hiesigen Agentur der Hamburg-Amerika
Linie mit den zuständigen kubanischen Stellen bis zum
heutigen Tage keinen Abschluss gefunden hatten, vor
allem aber, dass mir als dem Reichsvertreter von Seiten der kubanischen Regierung keinerlei definitive Entscheidung zur Kenntnis gebracht worden ist.

　　Zu der Frage der Nichtbeachtung der kubanischen
Einwanderungsbestimmungen durch die Agentur der Schiff-
fahrtsgesellschaft und die Passagiere darf ich bemerken,
dass der Generaldirektor der Immigration Herr Benitez
mit seinen offiziellen, in der Anlage abschriftlich
beigefügten Schreiben vom 9. v. Mts. den Agenten der

　　　　　　　　　　　　　　　　　　　__Hapag__

Hapag ausdrücklich mitgeteilt hat, dass die von ihm
vor dem 6. Mai ds. Js. ausgestellten Landungsgenehmigungen gültig sind. Auf welche Weise die von Herrn
Benitez erteilten Landungsgenehmigungen zustande gekommen sind, und woraufhin er diese Mitteilung an die
Agentur der Hapag gesandt hat, ist eine interne kubanische Angelegenheit und für die deutsche Schiffahrtsgesellschaft ohne Belang. Im übrigen hat das Staatssekretariat konsequenterweise die von den kubanischen
Konsuln ohne seine Ermächtigung erteilten Sichtvermerke
anerkannt, die Konsuln indessen, wie aus der Presse bekannt ist, zur Rechenschaft gezogen. Ein entsprechendes
Verfahren des Finanzministeriums gegenüber den ihm unter-
stellten Beamten, anlässlich der vor dem 6. ds. Mts. von
ihnen erteilten Landungsgenehmigungen, ist dagegen ausge-
blieben.

Ich bedaure aufrichtig, diese Note an Eure Exzellenz
richten zu müssen, sehe mich indessen angesichts der in
in Frage stehenden Dekret enthaltenen Gewaltandrohung
einem Schiff gegenüber, das unter der Flagge Deutschlands,
das ich hier zu vertreten die Ehre habe, fährt, hierzu
gezwungen.

Wenn auch die kubanische Regierung die Auffassung
vertritt, dass durch ein weiteres Verbleiben des Schiffes
"St. Louis" im Hafen von Habana die öffentliche Sicherheit des Landes gefährdet werden könnte, so erscheint
eine Gewaltandrohung dem deutschen Schiff gegenüber
hierdurch doch nicht berechtigt, umsoweniger als die
Agentur der Hapag keinerlei Veranlassung hierzu gegeben
hat.

111

                    gez:Kaempfe
                    Deutscher Geschäftsträger

Uebersetzung.

D E K R E T No.1168.

In Anbetracht dessen, dass das Dekret No.55 vom 13.Januar ds.Js., das in der Gaceta Oficial vom 26. veröffentlicht ist, im Artikel IV bestimmt, dass die Touristen von der Verpflichtung, den Garantiebetrag entsprechend Artikel II zu hinterlegen, ausgenommen sind und sie wie diejenigen Personen behandelt werden, die zum Vergnügen reisen und sich nicht irgendwelcher Arbeit widmen,

In Anbetracht dessen, dass der Artikel XI desselben Dekrets endgültig bestimmt, dass die Tatsache, von der Garantieleistung von 500 Pesos ausgenommen zu sein und die anderen verlangten Vorschriften erfüllt zu haben, die Reisenden nicht von der Verpflichtung der Visierung des Passes oder eines andern Ausweisdokuments befreie – mit Ausnahme der im Dekret No.2507 vom 17.November 1928 vorgesehenen Fälle,

In Anbetracht dessen, dass am 5.letzten Monats in der Gaceta Oficial das Dekret vom gleichen Datum No.937 veröffentlicht worden ist, in dem das vorherige dahin ergänzt wird, dass alle Touristen mit Ausnahme der Nordamerikaner verpflichtet sind, sich eine Erlaubnis des Staats- und Arbeitssekretariats zu beschaffen, die direkt und schriftlich von diesen Beamten den Schiffahrtsgesellschaften vor der Einschiffung des autorisierten Passagiers im Ursprungshafen mitzuteilen sind, diese Bedingungen überhaupt nicht beachtet worden sind, weder von Seiten der Schiffahrtsgesellschaft, der Eigentümerin des Schiffes "San Luis" noch von den erwähnten Passagieren,

In Anbetracht dessen, dass am 27. des laufenden (soll heissen "vergangenen") Monats das Schiff deutscher Flagge namens "San Luis" im Hafen von Habana eintraf, das am 13.Mai den Hafen von Hamburg, Deutschland, mit 936 Fahrgästen an Bord verlassen hatte, die sich gezwungen sahen, wegen politischer Probleme ihr ursprüngliches Vaterland zu verlassen, ohne dass der grösste Teil von ihnen die vorher aufgeführten Bestimmungen genau erfüllt hätte,

In Anbetracht dessen, dass die Eigenschaft als Tourist, die von ihnen beansprucht wird, nach jeder Richtung hin unstatthaft ist, weil bei richtiger Beurteilung, wie schon vorher festgestellt wurde, es nicht möglich ist, diese Eigenschaft bei Personen anzuwenden, die nicht zum Vergnügen reisen sondern sich durch höhere Gewalt gezwungen sehen, in Länder anzuwandern, in denen die Gründe, die ihre Auswanderung veranlassten nicht bestehen,

In Anbetracht dessen, dass auch bei grosszügiger Auslegung und in der Anerkennung ihrer Eigenschaft als Tourist von ihnen die Bedingung der Visierung der Pässe nicht erfüllt worden ist und damit offen der erwähnte Artikel XI des Dekrets 55 und der Absatz A des Artikels IV, so wie er durch Bestimmung 2 des Dekrets 937 vom 5.Mai 1939 abgefasst wurde, verletzt worden ist,

In Anbetracht dessen, dass durch die vorher aufgeführten Tatsachen greifbar nachgewiesen worden ist, dass die Bestimmungen über Einwanderung sowohl von den Passagieren, die sich noch an Bord des erwähnten Schiffes "San Luis" befinden, als auch von der Schiffahrtsgesellschaft, der Eigentümerin des Schiffs, umgangen worden sind, woraus klar hervorgeht, dass die Landung derselben in Uebereinstimmung mit den Anordnungen im ersten Paragraph des Teil II der Militärverfügung No.55 vom Jahre 1902 nicht erlaubt werden kann,

In

In Anbetracht dessen, dass das Verbleiben des erwähnten Schiffs
"San Luis" im Hafen von Habana und das Sichanbordbefinden
der 917 Personen, auf die sich die ursprüngliche Zahl ver-
ringert hat, weil die Ausschiffung von 18 von ihnen erlaubt
wurde, und weil andere in einem Hospital in der Stadt unter-
gebracht sind, eine tatsächliche Störung der öffentlichen
Sicherheit verursacht hat, die im Laufe der Stunden immer
grösser werden wird, durch welchen Zustand die Regierung
zur Vermeidung grösseren Unheils sich gezwungen sieht, aus-
sergewöhnliche Massnahmen zu ergreifen, um den augenblick-
lichen Zustand zu beenden und für die normale Abwicklung der
Bewegung im Hafen und der genauesten Erfüllung der gesetzlichen Vorschriften pflichtgemäss Sorge zu tragen,

             v e r o r d n e   i c h

von den mir gesetzlich zustehenden Befugnissen Gebrauch
machend und auf Grund der allgemeinen Zweckmässigkeit von mir
aus nach Kenntnisnahme des Gutachtens des Staatssekretärs des
Innern und auf Vorschlag des Staatssekretärs der Finanzen

ERSTENS: Herrn Luis Clasing in seiner Eigenschaft als Agent der
Hamburg-Amerika Linie, Eigentümerin des im Hafen liegenden
Schiffes, aufzufordern, dass er umgehend die nötigen Anordnungen gebe, damit das besagte Schiff "San Luis" am Tage der
Verfügung selbst mit allen Passagieren, die sich an Bord
befinden und deren Landung nicht erlaubt wurde, den Hafen
verlasse.

ZWEITENS: Für den Fall, dass besagter Agent sich weigern sollte,
diese Anordnungen zu geben, oder dass diese nicht am selben
Tage der Aufforderung ausgeführt werden würden, wird durch
das Finanzsekretariat die Hilfe der konstitutionellen Kriegsmarine angefordert werden, die das erwähnte Schiff "San Luis"
mit allen Passagieren an Bord ausserhalb der Hoheitsgewässer der
Nation bringen wird.

DRITTENS: Jedes Mitglied der Besatzung des erwähnten Schiffes, das
sich ungesetzlich an Land begeben haben sollte, wird fest-
genommen und von der Polizei an Bord des Schiffes gebracht
werden.

VIERTENS: Dass durch den Finanzminister und in Uebereinstimmung mit
den Vorschriften des Gesetzes über den Zivildienst die ent-
sprechenden Schritte eingeleitet werden, um die Verantwort-
lichkeiten zu bereinigen, die durch gewisse Beamte verursacht
sein könnten.

        Der Staatssekretär der Finanzen und der der National-
Verteidigung haben für die genaue Durchführung der gegebenen
Anordnung Sorge zu tragen.

        Gegeben im Präsidentenpalast in Habana am ersten Juni
1939.
                        gez. Präsident

        gez. Finanzsekretär.

113

Servicio de Aduana
Cuba.   ADUANA DE LA HABANA.

Negociado de
Correspondencia.   "SECCION DE ASUNTOS GENERALES"

_____

Habana, 1.Juni 1939.

Herrn Luis Clasing
Vertreter des Dampfers "San Luis"
der Hamburg-Amerika Linie
H a b a n a

Sehr geehrter Herr:

In Ausführung des Dekrets No. 1168 vom heutigen
Datum, das ich im Durchschlag beifüge, teile ich Ihnen mit,
dass der Dampfer "San Luis" in den ersten Morgenstunden des
heutigen Tages diesen Hafen verlassen muss, um sich nach
irgendeinem anderen Hafen des Auslands, der ihm gut erscheint,
zu begeben, ohne irgend eine Landung des Restes der an Bord
befindlichen Passagiere, die er nach hier brachte, zu unternehmen.

Der besondere Grund der öffentlichen Sicherheit hat
eine bevorzugte Beachtung vor der Einwanderungs-und Zollbe-
handlung. Er zwingt zur sofortigen Anwendung einer geeignet
erscheinenden Massnahme, damit die besagte Anordnung der
Regierung, in der Hauptsache auf Gründe der öffentlichen
Sicherheit gestützt, wie das erwähnte Präsidentialgesetz aus-
drückt, in unveränderlicher Form durchgeführt wird.

Ich mache Sie von vornherein auf die Konsequenzen
aufmerksam, die sich für das an Sie konsignierte Schiff er-
geben könnten, wenn die Massnahmen für die öffentliche Sicherheit, die von der Regierung angeordnet sind, nicht entsprechend ausgeführt werden.

Sie werden bevollmächtigt als Consignatär genannten
Schiffes und im Hinblick auf die Wichtigkeit der Massnahme die
sofortige Ausfahrt des Schiffs anzuornen, ohne irgendwelche
weiteren Handlungen zu unternehmen, und werden daraufhin
frei von jeder Verantwortlichkeit für Vergehen gegen die
Zollbestimmungen sein, die zurzeit in Kraft sind, andernfalls wird die Verantwortung auf Sie fallen. Diese Ausnahme

114

nahme versteht sich von selbst infolge des zwingenden
Charakters der von der Regierung für die öffentliche
Sicherheit getroffenen Massnahmen.

Ich bitte Sie, Einwendungen irgendwelcher Art,
die Sie zu machen hätten, schriftlich an den Unterzeichneten zu richten, weil ich diese Aufforderung an Sie
in Ausführung der genauen Bestimmungen der Regierung
selbst mache.

Ich bitte Sie, mir den Hafen im Auslande zu
nennen nach dem das Schiff fährt, um Ihnen die Erfüllung der gesetzlichen Bestimmungen hinsichtlich der Zoll-
angelegenheiten zu erleichtern.

Weiterhin bitte ich Sie, alles Notwendige, um
das Schiff in ausreisefähigen Zustand zu bringen, mit
der grössten Schnelligkeit zu beschaffen, einschliess-
lich der Verproviantierung, die der Kapitän für nötig
hält, da sonst andere Massnahmen den Entschluss der
Regierung von Kuba bekräftigen würden, der in diesen
Falle ja nichts anderes bezweckt, als dass das Schiff
den Hafen so schnell als möglich verlässt.

Ich bitte Sie, von diesem Entscheid Kenntnis zu
nehmen und den beiliegenden Durchschlag zu unterzeichnen
und mir zurückzuschicken ! Erleichtern Sie die ver-
langte Auskunft, treffen Sie die angeordneten notwendigen Massnahmen und kommen Sie den Anordnungen nach in
der dringlichen Frist, die der Charakter des Beschlusses
der Regierung betreffend die öffentliche Sicherheit verlangt.

115

Hochachtungsvoll

I.A. des Herrn Sekretärs
gez. Dr. Miguel A. Varona
Director Administrador.

Deutsche Gesandtschaft
Havana
(Legación Alemana)

———

T.Nr. 1150/39

Im Anschluss an den Bericht
vom 2.ds.Mts. - T.Nr. 1143/39 -

Inhalt: "San Luis" - Zwischenfall.

Habana, den 6.Juni 1939.

4 Anlagen.
15 Zeitungsausschnitte.

Im Anschluss an meinen obenbezeichneten Bericht beehre ich mich in den Anlagen Abschrift und Uebersetzung
einer an mich gerichteten Note des Staatssekretärs des
Auswärtigen, Dr.Remos, vom 5.ds.Mts. und meine Antwort-
note vom gleichen Datum zu übersenden.

Dr.Remos lässt sich in seiner Note weitschweifig über
die Frage der Unerwünschtheit der Juden in Cuba, was an
sich sehr erfreulich und verständlich ist, aus, erwähnt
unrichtigerweise wiederholt, dass die Juden von "San Luis"
aus Deutschland ausgewiesen (expulsado) worden seien,
nennt unüberzeugende und keinesfalls durchschlagende Gründe für die Nichtbeantwortung meiner Noten vom 10. und 23.
v.Mts., verfällt in chronologische Fehler und geht vor
allem auf den Kern der Angelegenheit, nämlich auf die dem
Schiff zu kurz gesetzte Frist für das Verlassen des Hafens
und auf die Gewaltandrohung, die für die Entsendung meiner
Note vom 1.ds.Mts. entscheidend waren, überhaupt nicht
ein. Ich habe mich deshalb veranlasst gesehen, ihm noch
vor Weiterleitung seiner Note an das Auswärtige Amt kurz
zu antworten und zu einzelnen seiner Behauptungen Stellung
zu nehmen.

Während ich in meinen Noten vom 10. und 23.v.Mts. auf
Antrag der hiesigen Hapag-Agentur und insbesondere aus dem
Gesichtspunkt heraus, dass die Rückkehr der Juden nach
Deutschland unerwünscht wäre, den Staatssekretär bat, den

Juden

An das
Auswärtige Amt,

B E R L I N .

Juden, die sich vor Inkrafttreten des Dekrets vom
5.v.Mts. eingeschifft haben oder vor dem gleichen
Datum ausgestellte Einreisegenehmigungen besitzen,
landen zu lassen, erwähnte ich in meiner Note vom
1.ds.Mts. die jüdischen Emigranten überhaupt nicht,
sondern wandte mich gegen die ungehörige Behandlung
eines deutschen Schiffs und gegen die Gewaltandrohung
seitens der Cubanischen Regierung. Selbstverständlich gab ich hierbei auch meiner Verwunderung darüber Ausdruck, dass das Staatssekretariat meine früheren Noten nicht beantwortet hat und mich als Reichsvertreter überhaupt ohne jede Information über die
gegen unser Schiff getroffenen Gewaltmassnahmen liess.

Jedenfalls war es m.E. durchaus richtig und erforderlich, bei der Cubanischen Regierung wegen ihres
ungehörigen Verhaltens Vorstellungen zu erheben und
ihr zu verstehen zu geben, dass Deutschland nicht ge-
willt ist, sich von ihr derartige Dinge gefallen zu
lassen. Im übrigen ist die recht konfuse Note des
Herrn Remos sehr weich abgefasst und lässt erkennen,
dass die Cubanische Regierung meinen Schritt ganz
richtig verstanden hat.

Wenn Herr Remos, was für uns natürlich sehr interessant ist, davon spricht, dass die Juden in Cuba
unerwünscht seien, und dabei hervorhebt, dass sie gerade in Deutschland als für das nationale Wohlergehen
schädliche Elemente angesehen werden, so entsprechen
seine Ausführungen nicht gerade den von dem Präsidenten Laredo Bru gestern Pressevertretern gegenüber gemachten Ausserungen, in denen er die Juden seiner auf-
richtigen und tiefen Anteilnahme versichert und erklärt,
dass die Cubanische Regierung im Zeichen der Weltbrüderlichkeit Massnahmen treffen werde, um für die Juden von "San Luis" in Cuba, voraussichtlich auf der
Isla de Pinos, ein Konzentrationslager einzurichten.
Hierfür verlangt er allerdings von dem jüdisch-amerikanischen Anwalt Berenson, über den ich bereits in

meinem

117

meinem letzten Bericht geschrieben habe, Garan-
tien dafür, dass diese Juden dem Staat nicht zur
Last fallen, und dass ihre Einschiffung und Ver-
sorgung für den Fall, dass sie die Erlaubnis nach
einem anderen Lande (Amerika) zu gehen erhalten,
sichergestellt sind. Dass bei dieser Selbstbeweih-
räucherung des Herrn Staatspräsidenten nicht die
Gefühle der Weltbrüderlichkeit, sondern ganz andere Gründe, die ich nicht näher bezeichnen möchte,
die Hauptrolle spielen, ist für jeden, der die
hiesigen Verhältnisse einigermassen kennt, voll-
kommen klar. Es erscheint durchaus wahrscheinlich, dass die cubanischen Bedingungen nicht so
hoch geschraubt sind, wie die der Dominikaner, über
deren Humanität und Anteilnahme für die armen, aus
Deutschland ausgewiesenen Juden, die Zeitungen in
den letzten Tagen geschrieben haben. Wie dem auch
sei, heute nachmittag soll die Entscheidung der Cubanischen Regierung über die Zulassung bezw. Nicht-
zulassung der "San Luis"-Juden fallen. Nach den
letzten Pressemitteilungen soll sich "San Luis" nicht,
wie die Hapag-Agentur mir versicherte, auf der Heim-
reise befinden, sondern sich unweit von Cuba aufhalten, um die Entscheidung der Cubanischen Regierung
abzuwarten. Noch am heutigen Abend wird wohl das
Ergebnis der zwischen der Cubanischen Regierung
und dem jüdisch-amerikanischen Anwalt Berenson ge-
führten Verhandlungen bekannt gegeben werden.

Wie ich von dem Kapitän des Hapag-Schiffs
"Iberia" neulich hörte, soll das Schwesterschiff
"Orinoco", das am 27.v.Mts. mit weiteren 200 Juden,
die keine gültigen cubanischen Einreisegenehmigungen hatten, Deutschland verliess, angesichts des
"San Luis"-Zwischenfalls diese wieder nach Hamburg
zurückgebracht haben. Ich kann dies nur begrüssen,
denn es liegt entschieden im Interesse der guten
deutsch-cubanischen Beziehungen, dass von nun ab
jüdische Emigranten, die die entsprechend dem letzten
Einwanderungsgesetz

Einwanderungsgesetz erforderlichen Einreisegenehmigungen nicht besitzen, auf deutschen Dampfern nicht mehr nach Cuba geschafft werden.

Abschliessend möchte ich darauf hinweisen, dass wenn auch der "San Luis"-Fall bedauerlicherweise nicht nur in Cuba, sondern auch in anderen Ländern, insbesondere in den Vereinigten Staaten von Amerika eine Pressehetze gegen Deutschland ausgelöst hat, er andererseits erneut gezeigt hat, dass die Juden auch in dieser Hemisphäre als unerwünschte Elemente betrachtet werden.

Eine Reihe von betreffenden Zeitungsausschnitten ist in der Anlage beigefügt.

Ueber setzung.

Republik Cuba.
STAATSSEKRETARIAT.
No.925.

La Habana, den 5.Juni 1939.

Herr Geschäftsträger,

Ich habe die Ehre Ihnen den Empfang Ihrer gefälligen Note vom 1.Juni zu bestätigen, in der Sie sich auf
das Dekret No.1168 und auf die peinliche Lage, in der
sich die Passagiere des deutschen Dampfers "San Luis"
befunden haben, als sie beabsichtigten ungesetzlich mit
Verletzung der für das Einwanderungswesen bestehenden Bestimmungen in Cuba hereinzukommen, sowie auch auf die
dringenden Massnahmen, die im Gebrauche seiner Befugnisse,
aber mit der für ein Schiff deutscher Flagge notwendigen
Rücksicht die Regierung der Republik zu treffen sich gezwungen gesehen hat, um dadurch das Hereinbringen von
unerwünschten Elementen in unser Land zu vermeiden.

120

Gestatten Sie mir bei der Beantwortung der erwähnten Note die Ueberraschung der cubanischen Regierung aus-
zudrücken, in erster Linie über die von den Konsignatären
des "San Luis" gemachten Bemerkungen über eine gesetzliche
Bestimmung der Regierung von Cuba, durch die sie sich
weigert, gewisse von Deutschland ausgewiesene Elemente
zuzulassen, die Ihre Regierung selbst als für das nationale Wohlergehen schädlich ansieht und denen sie,
abgesehen(?) von ihrer Abstammung nicht erlaubt, sich
länger in Deutschland aufzuhalten.

Dies ist der Grund, weshalb die Noten vom 10. und
23.vergangenen Monats, die dieses besondere Interesse
verteidigten und vermutlich ohne genügende Kenntnis der
Sachlage geschickt wurden, nicht rechtzeitig beantwortet
wurden und diese Gelegenheit benutzc, um den entsprechen-
den Empfang zu bestätigen.

An   Am

Herrn Dr.Walter Kaempfe,
Deutscher Geschäftsträger a.i.
HABANA.
================================

Am 17.Mai, also vor Abfahrt des Schiffs aus
europäischen Häfen hatte die Einwanderungsbehörde.
der Republik Herrn Luis Clasing unterrichtet, dass
der Cubanischen Regierung zu Ohren gekommen sei,dass
an Bord des Dampfers "San Luis" eine grosse Anzahl
von jüdischen Passagieren käme, und dass das Landen
von diesen in Cuba nicht erlaubt sei, es sei denn,
dass sie die Bestimmungen des Dekrets No.937 vom 5.
des laufenden(!) Monats erfüllten. Die Mitteilung
hierüber hat Herr Clasing, Konsignatär der Hamburg-
Amerika Linie, laut Empfangsbestätigung, die im Be-
sitze der Einwanderungsbehörde des Finanzsekretariats
ist, erhalten.

Die Behauptung, die Sie deshalb sicherlich auf
Auskunft des Herrn Clasing hin machen, dass der Generaldirektor der Einwanderungsbehörde an ihn am 9.des
vergangenen Monats ein offizielles Schreiben gerich-
tet und ihm darin mitgeteilt hatte, dass die von ihm
vor dem 6.Mai ausgestellten Landungsgenehmigungen
gültig wären, ist rechtzeitig durch die spätere Mitteilung vom 17. und vor der Abreise des "San Luis"
auf die ich mich oben beziehe, richtig gestellt
worden.

Glücklicherweise scheint aus Ihrer ausführlichen
Note nicht hervorzugehen, dass Ihre Regierung Sie beauftragt habe, diese ungerechtfertigte Vorstellung bei
der Cubanischen Regierung zu machen, sondern dem ohne
Zweifel anzuerkennenden Eifer zuzuschreiben ist, die
ungewöhnliche Handlungsweise einer Gesellschaft zu
erklären, die wenn sie auch deutsch ist, in Cuba ar-
beitet und versucht hat. die Bestimmungen, die in
dieser Nation für Einwanderungswesen bestehen, gewalt-
sam zu verletzen.

Wie Sie beim Lesen des Präsidentialdekrets No.
1168 bemerken können, hat die Cubanische Regierung
alle möglichen Nachforschungen angestellt, um die
Verantwortlichkeit festzustellen, die diejenigen haben könnten, die in diesem unangenehmen Vorfall mit
                                        beteiligt

beteiligt gewesen sind, kann aber ihre Befürchtung nicht verbergen, dass bei dieser Nach-
forschung ein schweres Verschulden auf die Ree-
derei des "San Luis" fällt, sei es wegen ihres
Einverständnisses mit Personen, die Interesse
haben, die Cubanische Regierung zu zwingen, in
ihrem Lande unerwünschte Elemente aufzunehmen,
sei es, weil sie den ausdrücklichen Warnungen
zuwiderhandeln, die rechtzeitig gegeben wurden,
um den Versuch, derartige unfreiwillige Einwanderer einzuführen, zu verhindern, deren Unerwünschtheit die Deutsche Regierung selbst anzu-
.erkennen scheint, dadurch, dass sie diese aus ihrem Lande ausweist, unabhängig von ihrer wirkli-
chen Abstammung, ein Grund, der gleichfalls die
Tatsache rechtfertigt, dass Ihnen die getroffenen
Massnahmen angesichts der Gefährdung der Sachlage
von den kubanischen Behörden nicht mitgeteilt wurden.

122

Weiterhin macht das Staatssekretariat, ohne
den Hinweis, den Sie sich betreffs der Untersu-
chungen der inneren Angelegenheiten, die die kubanische Regierung durchzuführen hätte, zurückzuweisen,
darauf aufmerksam, dass diese auf jeden Fall der
eignen Beurteilung hierüber unterliegen.

Um trotzalledem irgendwelchen Zweifel, den
Sie noch über die Intervention des Aussendienstes
Kubas in diesen Angelegenheiten haben könnten, zu
beseitigen, kann ich versichern, dass die ausgestellten Visas keine 20 sind, die in allen Fällen
in guter Absicht und aus vermutlicher Unkenntnis
der neuen durch das Dekret No. 937 geschaffenen Lage,
und dass schliesslich alle Personen, die ihre Pässe
mit dem ausgestellten Visum mit oder ohne Anordnung
dieses Staatssekretariats vorgezeigt haben, in der
richtigen Weise behandelt worden sind, und ihnen
das Landen in Cuba erlaubt wurde.

                                                Ich

Ich bedaure ausserordentlich, dass die Hart-
näckigkeit einer Gesellschaft, die in diesem Fall
genau wusste, dass sie, wenn sie in Kuba auf
eigne Faust hin aus Deutschland ausgewiesene Juden einführen wollte, gegen die kubanischen Gesetze
verstiess, zu einem peinlichen Vorfall zwischen der
Vertretung Deutschlands in Kuba und dieser Regierung
Anlass gegeben hat, die die äusserst herzlichen Beziehungen mit dem Deutschen Reich unverletzt aufrecht
zu erhalten und jeden Tag mehr zu entwickeln wünscht.

Ich benutze diese Gelegenheit . . . .

gez: Remos.

123

Herr Sekretär:

Mit verbindlichstem Dank beehre ich mich Euer
Exzellenz den Empfang der sehr gefälligen Note von heute Nr. 925 zu bestätigen und möchte nicht verfehlen, zunächst das Nachstehende zu bemerken:

1. Wenn Eure Exzellenz in der oben genannten Note wiederholt davon sprechen, dass die mit dem Schiff "San Luis"
   seinerzeit gebrachten Juden aus Deutschland ausgewiesen
   worden seien, so ist dies nicht zutreffend. Die in Frage stehenden Juden haben Deutschland freiwillig verlassen.

2. Dass der Herr Generaldirektor Benitez mit seinem Schreiben vom 9. vor. Mts. die Hapag-Agentur offiziell hat
   wissen lassen, dass die von ihm vor dem 6. vor. Mts.
   ausgestellten Einreisegenehmigungen gültig sind, ist eine
   unbestreitbare Tatsache, und musste von der Hapag-Agentur
   als ein amtlicher Bescheid betrachtet werden.

3. Das Schiff "San Luis" hat Hamburg am 13. vor. Mts. verlassen, also nicht nach, sondern vor der Absendung des
   von Euer Exzellenz erwähnten Schreibens vom 17. vor. Mts.
   an die Hapagagentur.

4. Eure Exzellenz erwähnen mit keinem einzigen Wort die Punkte
   meiner durchaus berechtigt gewesenen Note vom 1. ds. Mts.,
   die den Kern der Angelegenheit bilden und überhaupt die
   Veranlassung zur Absendung derselben gewesen sind, nämlich die im Dekret vom 1. ds. Mts. Nr. 1168 für die Verproviantierung des vollbesetzten grossen Schiffs zu kurz
   gesetzte Frist zum Verlassen des Hafens und vor allem die
   Drohung, das Schiff, falls es nicht rechtzeitig den Hafen
   von Habana verlassen sollte, durch die kubanische Kriegsmarine, also durch Gewalt, ausserhalb der Hoheitsgewässer
   Kubas hinauszugeleiten.

An Seine Exzellenz
    Herrn Dr. Juan J. Remos,
        Staatssekretär des Aeusseren
            H a b a n a .

Im vorliegenden Fall handelt es sich nicht um die
jüdischen Emigranten aus Deutschland und die Frage, ob sie
für Kuba erwünschte oder unerwünschte Elemente darstellen,
sondern einzig und allein um die Behandlung eines deutschen
Schiffs durch die kubanische Regierung, die nicht nur für
die deutsche Schiffahrt, sondern auch für Deutschland selbst,
das ich hier zu vertreten die Ehre habe, verletzend ist.

Ich werde die sehr gefällige Note Euer Exzellenz in Abschrift meiner Regierung übermitteln und ihre Instruktionen
abwarten.

Zum Schluss möchte ich Euer Exzellenz versichern, dass
es auch mein heisser und aufrichtiger Wunsch und mein
Bestreben ist, die guten Beziehungen zwischen Kuba und
Deutschland zu fördern und zu vertiefen, dass es indessen
auch meine Pflicht als Reichsvertreter ist, die mir richtig
erscheinden Schritte g gen Deutschland verletzende Massnahmen zu unternehmen.

Ich benutze . . . .

125

gez: Kaempfe.

**Deutsche Gefandtſchaft
Havana**

· (Legación Alemana)

T.Nr.1157/39

Im Anschluss an den Bericht
vom 6.ds.Mts. – T.Nr.1150/39 –

Inhalt: "San Luis"-Zwischenfall.

Habana, den 7.Juni 1939.

Die Verhandlungen, die der jüdisch-amerikanische
Anwalt Lawrence Berenson mit der Cubanischen Regierung geführt hat, sind gestern gescheitert. Der Präsident der Republik hat den Vorschlag des Juden, wonach Cuba einen
Garantiebetrag von $ 443 000.- für die Emigranten von
"San Luis", vom englischen Schiff "Orduña" (72 Personen)
und vom französischen Schiff "Flandre" (85 Personen) erhalten sollte, abgelehnt und die Landung all dieser Juden
definitiv verboten.

Der wenig schöne Kuhhandel, bei dem die jüdischen
Organisationen den von Cuba verlangten, zu hoch ange-
setzten Geldbetrag für die Aufnahme der Juden nicht be-
willigen wollten, hat, nachdem er die Oeffentlichkeit
der hiesigen Hemisphäre längere Zeit beschäftigt hat,
sein Ende gefunden. Das Schiff "San Luis" hat nunmehr,
da weder Cuba, noch Santo Domingo, noch die Vereinigten
Staaten, an deren Präsidenten sich die Juden zuletzt telegraphisch gewandt hatten, sie aufgenommen haben, auf
Anordnung der Hapag Kurs nach Europa genommen und be-
findet sich auf der Rückreise nach Hamburg.

Während der Vorfall für die jüdischen Emigranten
beendet zu sein scheint, kann dies in Bezug auf die unerhörte Behandlung des Schiffs "San Luis" durch die Cubanische Regierung nicht behauptet werden. Ich darf erneut
meiner Meinung dahin Ausdruck geben, dass Deutschland
das unerhörte Verhalten der Cubaner unter Protest zurück-
weisen muss. Für eine möglichst baldige Weisung entsprechend meinen Berichten vom 2. und vom 6.ds.Mts. – T.Nr.
1143/39 und 1150/39 – wäre ich deshalb dankbar.

An das
    Auswärtige Amt,
        B E R L I N .

126

zu 83-26 2/6., 6/6., 7/6. und 20/6.

Aus dem anliegenden Bericht aus Antwerpen
vom 20.d.M. geht hervor, daß die 907 jüdischen Passagiere der "St.Louis" die das Schiff in Habana nicht
verlassen durften,in Antwerpen ausgeschifft wurden.
Dies wird auch durch den anliegenden Aufsatz aus
dem"Jüdischen Nachrichtenblatt"vom 27.Juni bestä-
tigt, der Belgien, Holland, Frankreich und England als Aufnahmeländer nennt. Die Hapag hat
fernmündlich mitgeteilt, daß ihr durch die Angelegenheit kein finanzieller Schaden entstanden sei.
Von allen jüdischen Auswanderern lasse sie sich
grundsätzlich eine Sicherheitsleistung in Höhe
der Rückpassage zahlen, an die sie sich auch im
vorliegenden Falle gehalten habe.

Die Vorfälle in Habana hat unser dortiger
Geschäftsträger durch Noten bei der Kubanischen
Regierung zur Sprache gebracht und auf die ungehö-
rige Behandlung des deutschen Schiffes (zu kurze
Frist für das Verlassen des Hafens, wodurch die
Verproviantierung erschwert wurde) und auf die Ge-
waltandrohung (das Schiff sollte durch kubanische
Marine dazu gezwungen werden, falls es den Hafen
nicht rechtzeitig verließ) hingewiesen. In seinem
Bericht bittet der Geschäftsträger, daß gegen das
ungehörige Vorgehen der Kubanischen Regierung
offiziell

127

offizielle protestiert werden möchte. Er schreibt:

"Es wäre kaum etwas einzuwenden gewesen, wenn
die hiesige Regierung ohne Gewaltandrohung
das von den Juden vollbesetzte Schiff ver-
anlaßt hätte, den Hafen in angemessener Zeit
zu verlassen. Die Art, wie die Regierung ein
deutsches Schiff zu behandeln gewagt hat, hat
indessen mit Juden nichts mehr zu tun und
stelle eine Beleidigung Deutschlands dar,
die wir von Cuba, das schon wiederholt seine
antideutsche Einstellung offenbart hat, nicht
stillschweigend hinnehmen können."

Ref. Deutschland schließt sich der Auffassung des Geschäftsträgers, die auch von W IX geteilt wird, an.

Hiermit

        bei Pol.   mit der Bitte um Übernahme
und dem Anheimstellen der weiteren Veranlassung
vorgelegt. Es darf angeregt werden, den Protest
hier in Berlin dem kubanischen Geschäftsträger
gegenüber vorzubringen.

                Berlin, den 30. Juni 1939.

                                        Der deutsche

Der deutsche Geschäftsträger in Havana geht wohl zu
weit, wenn er das Verhalten der kubanischen Hafenbehörden
gegenüber dem Motorschiff "San Luis" als schwere Beleidigung
Deutschlands bezeichnet. Andererseits steht auch Pol IX auf
dem Standpunkt, daß wir die Maßnahmen der Kubanischen Regierung nicht ohne weiteres hinnehmen sollen, wenn sie auch
wohl im wesentlichen durch den Wunsch diktiert waren, die
Landung unerwünschter Elemente zu verhindern. Es wird infolgedessen vorgeschlagen, der Kubanischen Regierung in einer
Note unser Befremden über diese Maßnahmen zum Ausdruck zu
bringen und dagegen Verwahrung einzulegen, allerdings ohne
durch den Ton der Note zu einer weiteren Verschärfung der
Beziehungen beizutragen. Der Protest selbst wird zweckmäßig
vom Schiffahrtsreferat (VLR Bleyert) formuliert, da es sich
bei den von uns beanstandeten Maßnahmen der Kubanischen Regierung um technische Schiffahrtsfragen (zu kurze Frist für
Verproviantierung, Drohung, das Schiff aus dem Hafen heraus-
zuschleppen usw.) handelt. Ein Protest bei dem hiesigen
kubanischen Geschäftsträger kommt nach Lage der Sache nicht
in Frage. Eine Übernahme der Angelegenheit im jetzigen Sta-
dium in das Ref. Pol IX wird nicht für zweckmäßig gehalten.

Hiermit

           dem Ref. Deutschland

wieder vorgelegt.

           Berlin, den 4. Juli 1939.

129

Berlin, den 3| Juli 1939.

83-26 22

An

die Hamburg-Amerika-Linie
z.Hd. von Herrn Direktor
Henning von Meibom,

Berlin N.8
Unter den Linden 61

Sehr geehrter H.Dir.v.Meibom,
Im Anschluß an mein Schreiben vom
6.v.M. -83-26 2/6.- darf ich Ihnen mitteilen, daß das AA. die Deutsche Gesandtschaft
in Havana nochmals angewiesen hat, gegen die
Behandlung des Hapagdampfers St.Louis,
der jüdische Auswanderer in Kuba landen
wollte, formell Protest zu erheben mit der
Begründung, daß die Reichsregierung die
Behandlung des Hapagschiffes St.Louis durch
die kubanischen Behörden als eine Verletzung
internationaler Verkehrsregeln sowie Nicht-
achtung der deutschen Flaggenehre zurückwei-
sen müsse.

Ich möchte annehmen, daß die Kubanische Regierung den Zwischenfall nunmehr in
einer zufriedenstellenden Weise erledigen
wird.

Heil Hitler !
(Schumburg)

bei

Pol. IX
W IX Schiff.

z. Mitz.

nach Abg:
Herrn Pldt
z.K.

130

Eingeg. am 31. Jul. 1939
gef. am 31.7.
gel. am 31.4.
abgesandt am 1. Aug. 1939

Habana, den 27.Juli 1939.

T.Nr.1461/39

Auf die anderweitige Weisung
vom 20.ds.Mts. - No.39 -

Inhalt: Protesterklärung wegen Behandlung
Hapag-Schiffs " St.Louis".

2 Anlagen.

131

Weisungsgemäss habe ich dem Staatssekretär Campa
die abschriftlich beigefügte Note nebst spanischer
Uebersetzung übergeben und dabei mündlich nachdrück-
lichst der Erwartung Ausdruck gegeben, dass die cubanische Regierung den Zwischenfall mit dem Hapag-Schiff
"St.Louis" in einer für Deutschland zufriedenstellenden
Form erledigen werde.

Herr Campa, der zur Zeit des Vorfalls noch nicht
Staatssekretär war - die unerhörte Behandlung des
Schiffs war dem inzwischen ausgeschiedenen, absolut
deutschfeindlichen Staatssekretär Remos zu verdanken -
hat mir sofort nach Durchsicht der Note sein aufrichti-
ges Bedauern über die seinerzeitige Behandlung des
Schiffs ausgesprochen, daraufhingewiesen, dass die Protesterklärung ihm als dem neuen Aussenminister äusserst
peinlich sei, und dass er nur den einen Wunsch hege,
zu Deutschland, dem er grosse Sympathie entgegenbringe,
die freundschaftlichsten und herzlichsten Beziehungen
zu unterhalten. Ich hatte aus seinen Worten und aus
der ganzen Art seines Verhaltens den festen Eindruck,
dass er die Behandlung des Schiffs durch die frühere
cubanische Regierung tatsächlich missbillige, und erklärte ihm, dass ich von der Aussprache seines Bedauerns
Kenntnis genommen hätte und meiner Regierung entsprechend berichten würde.

Zur Bekräftigung seines bereits ausgesprochenen
Bedauerns sandte Herr Campa heute früh noch den Chef

des

An das

Auswärtige Amt,

B E R L I N .

des Protokolls zu mir in die Gesandtschaft und
liess ihn erneut sein persönliches und der cubanischen Regierung Bedauern über die seinerzeitige
Behandlung des Schiffs aussprechen. Ich glaube,
dass die Form, in der Herr Campa den Vorfall erledigt hat, als zufriedenstellend angesehen werden dürfte, und dass wir auf eine weitere Verfol-
gung der Angelegenheit verzichten können.

132

TELEGRAM RECEIVED

JR   1—1336   **FROM**   GRAY

London

Dated June 13, 1939

Rec'd 12:35 p.m.

Secretary of State,

    Washington.

822, June 13, 5 p.m.

FROM PELL.

My 820, June 12, 7 p.m.

Doc. 5

    I obtained confirmation from the Dutch and Belgian

    133

Governments this morning that they would receive each

approximately two hundred of the ST. LOUIS passengers.

The French confirmed their decision to receive a like

number to Emerson who is in Paris and the Foreign

Office now states that the British Government will

act favorably on the recommendation that about three

hundred be received here. The passengers will be

landed at Southampton and from there directed to their

various destinations.

KENNEDY

HPD

TELEGRAM RECEIVED

1—1336

FROM

CJ

GRAY

LONDON

Dated June 14, 1939

Rec'd 2:25 p.m.

Secretary of State,

Washington.

Doc. 6

134

830, June 14, 8 p.m.

FROM PELL.

My 822, June 13, 5 p.m.

Arrangements have now been completed for the
ST. LOUIS to proceed to Antwerp, where the selection of
the various contingents will be made on board. The
Belgian and Netherlands contingents will be disembarked
and the French and British contingents transferred by
tender to a smaller vessel of the Hamburg-Amerika Line
which will take them to a French and British port at
the expense of the line.

KENNEDY

H PD

DEPARTMENT OF STATE

THE UNDER SECRETARY

November 18, 1939

RA - Mr. Briggs:

Please draft some appropriate reply to Professor Jessup for my signature and have drafted such instructions to the Embassy as may in your judgment be appropriate.

Doc. 7

135

U:BW:IJ

Columbia University
in the City of New York

SCHOOL OF LAW

November 17, 1939

The Honorable Sumner Welles
Under Secretary of State
Washington, D. C.

Dear Mr. Secretary:

I am writing you in a matter of some urgency
which has been brought to my attention by the National
Refugee Service. You probably recall that before his
departure for England, Professor Joseph P. Chamberlain
acted for some time as chairman of the board of this
organization. Upon his departure from the country, he
asked me to advise with them should any difficulties arise.

The matter involves the report of a proposed
amendment to the Cuban immigration law and would have the
result of confiscating moneys deposited as cash bonds
for refugees in Havana. We do not have exact figures but
I understand that some 3500 refugees are registered and
that for most of them a $500 bond has been deposited.
A large part of the money came through the National
Refugee Service, having been deposited with that organization by American citizens relatives of refugees in Cuba.

In some instances, cash bonds were put up by this organization where the refugee had no relatives in the United States.

I am informed that the proposed amendment to the Cuban immigration law is about to be introduced by Senator Gainas. I am also informed that he and Senator Casanova have stated that they will not introduce the bill unless President Laredo Bru approves. I am further informed that President Bru and his group are at present undecided concerning the enactment of this measure.

I believe that Mr. Warren of the Visa Division is familiar with the case and so is Consul General Du Bois. I am also informed that the matter has been brought to the attention of Ambassador Wright.

Since it appears from the information at my disposal that this is a project which would involve the confiscation of property of American citizens, I earnestly hope that you will ask for a report from Havana and if the facts are as reported to me, that urgent representations will be made to the Cuban Government.

Thanking you for your courtesy in giving your attention to this matter, I am

Sincerely yours,

My dear Professor Jessup:

I acknowledge the receipt of your letter of November 17 concerning the report of a proposed amendment to the Cuban immigration law which would have the result of confiscating the amounts deposited as cash bonds for refugees who have entered Cuba.

I am sending a copy of your letter to the American Ambassador in Habana with a request that he investigate this situation and report to me in regard thereto.

I appreciate your courtesy in writing me concerning this matter. With best regards, I am,

Sincerely yours,

Professor Philip C. Jessup,

School of Law,

Columbia University,

New York, New York.

RA:PWB:MJC   11-20-39

No. *1195*

To the American Ambassador,

Habana.

The Secretary of State transmits herewith a copy
of a letter dated November 17, 1939, from Professor
Philip C. Jessup of the School of Law of Columbia
University, to the Under Secretary of State, with
regard to the report of a proposed amendment to the
Cuban Immigration Law which would have the result of
confiscating the amounts deposited as cash bonds for
refugees entering Cuba. The Ambassador is requested to
investigate the situation described by Professor Jessup
and to inform the Department in regard thereto. An
instruction dated November 16, 1939 was addressed to
the Consul General regarding this subject.

139

Enclosure:

    Copy of letter from
    Professor Jessup,
    dated November 17, 1939.

PWB

RA:PWB:MJC   11-20-39

83-24 27/9.
9/11.
12/11.

Jüdische Emigranten auf in Riga
liegendem Dampfer "Manzoni."

D3-96

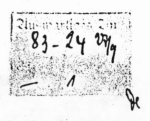

Telegramm (Gen.Ch.-Verf.)
Madrid, den 27 September 1939
Nr 1300 vom 27.9.   Berlin an, den 28.September 1 Uhr 45

Auf deutschem Dampfer Wangoni bekanntlich etwa
41 jüdische Emigranten, denen Einreise nach Sudan bewilligt worden war. Anheimstelle, durch Schweizerische
Vertretung London Engländern Weitertransport nahezule-
gen oder sonstwie Weiterreise eventuell über Portugal
zu ermöglichen, da sonst große Unterhaltsgelder und
unter Umständen hier Unruheherde entstehen

von Stohrer

141

Hergestellt in 13 St.
Davon sind gegangen:

Nr. 1 an Dtschl. (Arb.St.)
„ 2 „ R.A.M.
„ 3 „ St.S.
„ 4 „ Chef A.O.
„ 5 „ B.R.A.M.
„ 6 „ Dir. Pers.
„ 7 „ „ Pol.
„ 8 „ D.f. Pol.
„ 9 „ Dir. W
„ 10 „ „ Recht
„ 11 „ „ Presse
„ 12 „ „ Kult
„ 13 „ pers. Stab (Hewel)

Fibo bei Fbr.

83-24

Berlin, den   September 1959.   su 83-24, 27/9.

D i p l o g e r m a

B r ü s s e l

Nr.v... 341   <u>Telegramm in Ziffern:</u>

                               (Geh.Ch.Verf.)

                     Botschaft Madrid berichtet,dass auf
                     deutschem Dampfer **W a n g o n i** in Vigo
                     41 jüdische Emigranten, denen von Eng-
                     lischer Regirung Einreise nach Sudan
                     bewilligt.   Bitte van Zeeland als
                     Präsident Evian-Komittes ersuchen,
                     auf Englische Regierung wegen Weiterreise
                     eventuell über Portugal einzuwirken.

142   Schumburg

b Abgang:

     Pol. II Belg.

        Spanien

      W IX Schiffr.

      W XI

   zur Kts.

   ─────────────

D.Wangoni = gehört der Woermannlinie,die
ich nach fernmündl.Mitteilung von Hn.Geh.Rat
ieße (W XI) bereits mit dem Reichsbund der Juden (?)
egen der 41 Juden in Verbindung gesetzt hat.
 oermann-Linie: Herr Merkens,Tel.11 1903)

Auswärtiges Amt
83 - 24 5/10
eing. - OKT. 1939
1 Anl. 1 Durchschl.

Telegramm

(Geh.Ch.V.)

Brüssel, den 5. Oktober 1939 19.42 Uhr
Ankunft 5. " " ~~8.16~~ "
21.15

Nr. 254 vom 5.10.

auf Telegramm vom 30. Nr. 341 x)
x) 83 - 24 27.9.

Van Zeeland nach Amerika unterwegs, Schritte bei ihm waren daher nicht möglich. Sonstige Einwirkungsmöglichkeiten auf Evian-Komitee hier nicht gegeben.

Bargen.

Hergestellt in 2 Stücken.

Davon sind gegangen:

Nr. 1 an D.II (Arb.-St.)
" 2 " ~~RM.~~
" ~~3 " St.S.~~
" 4 " Chef A.O.
" 5 " B.R.M.
" 6 " Dir. Pers.
" 7 " Dir. Pol.
" 8 " Dg. Pol.
" 9 " Dir. W.
" 10 " Dg. W.
" 11 " Dir. Recht
" 12 " Dg. Recht
" 13 " Dir. Kult.
" 14 " Dg. Kult.
" 15 " Dir. Presse
" 16 " Abt. Prot.
" ~~17 " Ref. Deutschl.~~

Dies ist Nr. 1

SEA · LETTER

SPEEDED ON BY MAIL

RCA SHIP-TO-SHORE

Via RCA

837.55 ĪĠ/19

ĪM/HM

RECD FROM S.S. ORDUNA

KQ180/1 GLTS 87 SLT

FILED DATE 5/29/39

RECEIVED
DEPARTMENT OF STATE

JUN 10 1939 PM 2

COMMUNICATIONS
AND RECORDS

RECD AT CHATHAM MASS

VISA DIVISION

JUN 2 1939

Department of State

PRESIDENT ROOSEVELT

WASHINGTON DC

MR PRESIDENT WE ARE 72 REFUGEES FROM AUSTRIA CZECHOSLOVAKIA GERMANY NON ENGLISH

STEAMER ORDUNA IN SPITE OF LANDING PERMITS FROM THE DEPARTMENTO DIMMIGRACION

CUBA LANDING WAS REFUSED 27TH MAY WE ARE FORCED TO CONTINUE VOYAGE DIRECTION

SOUTHAMERICA AND PERHAPS BACK TO EUROPE STOP 67 OF US HAVE EITHER AFFIDAVITS

OR REGISTRATION NUMBERS FOR USA AND MEAN TO WAIT FOR THEIR AMERICAN VISAS AT

CUBA STOP IN THE NAME OF ALL WE ASK FOR HELP CONFIDING IN YOUR HUMANITY

DR RABBI TROESLER.
PINKUS HEPNER.

A 'SPECIAL RATE' RADIOGRAM RADIOED FROM SHIP-TO-SHORE & FORWARDED TO DESTINATION BY MAIL

Radiogram reply should be filed at any R.C.A. or Western Union Office

RADIOMARINE CORPORATION OF AMERICA ▸ 75 VARICK STREET, NEW YORK CITY

Abschrift!

Geheime Staatspolizei   Aachen, den 4.November 1941.
Staatspolizeistelle Aachen.
II B 3 - 675/41 g.
                                    G e h e i m !   S20
                                    Schnellbrief.

An die Herren Landräte des Bezirks pp.
                                    B 3944

Betrifft: Auswanderung von Juden.
Bezug: Ohne.

        Der Reichsführer ⚡⚡ und Chef der Deutschen Polizei hat ange-
ordnet, daß die Auswanderung von Juden mit sofortiger Wirkung zu
verhindern ist.

        Lediglich in ganz besonders gelagerten Einzelfällen z.B.bei
Vorliegen eines positiven Reichsinteresses, kann nach vorheriger Her-
beiführung der Entscheidung des Reichssicherheitshauptamtes der Auswanderung einzelner Juden stattgegeben werden.

        Ich ersuche, die Ortspolizeibehörden und Standesämter von dort
aus zu unterrichten.

                        In Vertretung:
                        gez.Schwitzgebel.
                  - - - - - -

Doc. 10

145

Der Landrat des Landkreises Aachen.   Aachen, den 5.November 1941.
Hauptbüro G.300/41 (g).
                        Geheim

        An die
        Herren Bürgermeister
                des K r e i s e s .

        Abschrift übersende ich zur Kenntnis und Beachtung.
Gleichzeitig ersuche ich, die Standesbeamten entsprechend zu
verständigen.
                  ────────────
        Abschrift übersende ich zur gefl.Kenntnis.
                        In Vertretung:
                        gez.Simon.
                        Beglaubigt:

An
den Herrn Landrat -Kommunalaufsicht-

        h i e r .
                        Reg.-Inspektor.

STAFF EVIDENCE ANALYSIS, Ministries Division.

By: Mark Schafer
Date: 15 May 1947

Document Number: NG - 1780

Title and/or general nature: Secret note from PAUSCH to EICH-
                                    MANN, stating that the German
                                    Embassy in Sofia reports that the
                                    Bulgarian Government has acceded to
                                    Germany's wishes to put the biggest
                                    obstacles in the way of Jewish
                                    transports to Palestine.

Form of Document: Typescript

Stamps and other endorsements: Handwritten notations and initial
                                    by RADEMACHER. Initials by PAUSCH.

Date: 26 March 1943

Doc. 11

146

Source: Inl. IIg Judenausreise nach
                                    Palestina 436777
                                    now at: FOSD, Bldg. 32 MDB, Berlin.
                                    (OCC BBT 1938)

PERSONS OR ORGANIZATIONS IMPLICATED:
                                    von THADDEN (indirectly)
                                    EICHMANN
                                    PAUSCH
                                    RADEMACHER (indirectly)

TO BE FILED UNDER THESE REFERENCE HEADINGS:
                                    NG - Foreign Office
                                    NG - Racial and Political
                                         Persecution
                                    NG - Atrocities

SUMMARY:
        The Foreign Office reports to EICHMANN of the RSHA, (Central
Reich Security Office) that the Bulgarian Government has
promised the German Embassy in Sofia (Ambassador BECKERLE) to
put all possible obstacles in the path of a migration of Jewish
children through Bulgaria to Palestine. Similar steps have been
taken by the German authorities in Roumania, urging the government
to try everything to prevent the escape of Jewish children to
Palestine.

E N D

26. März 1943

D III 403 g
Auswanderung von Juden aus Rumänien, auf
Schnellbr.v.10.3.43 Nr.IV B 3349/42 g -.

        Die Gesandtschaft Sofia hat mitgeteilt, dass die
Bulgarische Regierung unserem Wunsche, der etwaigen
Durchreise jüdischer Transporte nach Palästina durch
Bulgarien die grössten Schwierigkeiten entgegenzu-
setzen, entsprechen wird. Es ist jedoch noch unbekannt,
ob nicht trotzdem damit gerechnet werden muss, dass
einige Judentransporte durch Bulgarien durchkommen.
Die Angelegenheit wird im Auge behalten.

        Auch bei der Rumänischen Regierung sind entspre-
chende Vorstellungen erhoben worden, die Ausreise zu
verhindern. Es ist jedoch noch fraglich, ob und in-
wieweit diese Schritte Erfolg haben können.

147

Im Auftrag

An das
Reichssicherheitshauptamt
z.Hd.v.Obstubaf. Eichmann
Berlin W 35
Kurfürstenstr. 116

INTERGOVERNMENTAL COMMITTEE ON REFUGEES
Room 208,   1344 Connecticut Avenue, N.W.
Washington 25, D. C.

REFUGEE CHILDREN IN FRANCE, BELGIUM AND SWITZERLAND
X
Memorandum prepared by Sir Herbert W. Emerson
Director, Intergovernmental Committee on Refugees
11 December 1944

1.   During the occupation of France and Belgium, very fine work was
done by a number of agencies inside those countries, and in Switzerland,
towards the rescue of children whose parents were deported by the Nazis,
or had to flee from Nazi persecution.   It is feared that many of the parents h
have been killed.   The persecution was not confined to Jews, but was almost
univeral in their case, and was of a particularly brutal character.   During
our recent visit to France, Belgium and Switzerland, Dr. Kullmann and I
investigated, so far as we could, the problem of the Jewish children, with
special reference to the necessity of assistance by the Intergovernmental
Committee and the means by which such assistance might best be given.
While, owing to lack of communications and other causes, completely accu-
rate facts and figures are not yet available, the position is sufficiently
clear to give a general picture of the size and nature of the problem.

2.   The children now in question are those who were separated during
the occupation from both their parents.   The majority of them were concealed
under false names and papers in their own countries, and were maintained in
private families or in religious institutions.   The Churches gave great
assistance.   There were secret organizations operating in the countries,
and also from Switzerland.   The movement was financed partly by private
contributions, but largely by the Joint Distribution Committee of America.
In the later stages, the Intergovernmental Committee was able to give some
financial assistance through the Joint Distribution Committee, which acted
as its agent.   In Belgium, the Belgian authorities gave a good deal of
secret financial help.   Some children were removed to Switzerland, which
at the time of liberation, was giving asylum to about 1,000.   the number
there is now slightly less, since some children have been able to return to
France.

3.   The great majority of the Jewish children fall into three classes:-
       (i) The children of Belgian or French nationals.
       (ii) The children of other nationals, mainly Poles, who have been long
            established in France or Belgium.
       (iii) The children of refugees from Nazi persecution, mainly of German
            and Austrian origin, who had been given temporary asylum in
            France or Belgium.

In addition to the children of refugee parents, the mandate clearly
includes those children who had to be removed to Switzerland.   Moreover,

when, as was frequently the case, the situation of the children was a direct
consequence of the deportation or flight of their parents from their country
of residence, it would seem ungenerous to hold that the children should be
excluded from the benefits of the mandate merely on the ground that in
order to save their lives, they did not in fact leave their countries of
residence. I would hope, therefore, that when the time comes to consider
what practical help the Intergovernmental Committee can give towards a solution of this problem, the Executive Committee will approve a broad int er-
pretation of the mandate.

4. The figures so far ascertained are approximately as follows:-

(i) France - 8,000 children.
    Figures are not available for the distribution of these among the
    three classes mentioned in paragraph 3 above, but it is probable
    that the majority of them are children of Polish parents long
    established in France. There may be as many as 500 children of
    German and Austrian refugees.

(ii) Belgium - About 1,500 children were concealed who had neither parent
    with them. Of these a considerable proportion are children of
    German and Austrian refugees, the rest being mainly children of
    Polish parents long established in Belgium.

(iii) Switzerland
    About 1,000 divided among the three classes.

149

5. The Jewish community, as a whole, is giving very serious thought to
the future of these children. There are certain organizations which
took a very active part in their rescue and preservation. Such as the Comite
de Defense in Belgium and the OSE, operating mainly from Switzerland. The
Joint Distribution Committee is very closely interested because of the
financial help it has already given, and the still greater help it may be
called upon to give. The Jewish Agency for Palestine is prepared to make
a considerable number of certificates available for immigration into Palestine. The French Government has in contemplation a general scheme relating
to the welfare of war orphans, among whom most of the children now in question
would be included. Under this scheme the French Government would be the
legal guardian of the children, and would apparently provide for their
maintenance, welfare and education. The Belgian Government may consider a
similar scheme, although we have no definite information on this point.
The Swiss Government contemplates the return of the children now in
Switzerland to the countries from which they were received, but it has no
wish to make this an immediate issue, and is prepared to continue the/care
                                                                    the
and maintenance of them for the time being. Among the children are some who
have reached an age when they are capable of making up their own minds as to
what they wish their future to be. We were told, for instance, of 500
in Switzerland who have long made their plans to go to Palestine. About
them there is no difference of opinion between the various Jewish interest.
It is agreed that these youths should decide for themselves. About the
others, the present attitude of the organizations which have been directly
concerned with their rescue and preservation, is that no final decision
about the future of a child should ordinarily be made until every reasonable
effort has been made to trace one or both of his parents. Very good progress

has been made in this direction. In France, for instance, 2,500 children
have been united since liberation with one or both of their parents, and
500 more are in process of being united. There is also at present a strong
feeling among the organizations mentioned that provision should be made in
France or Belgium, as the case may be, for the care, education, maintenance
and training of many of the children. In France several homes previously
in existence have been re-opened for the purpose, and others are in contemplation. Until the details of the scheme of the French Government are known
the Jewish community is not in a position to form an opinion as to how far
will assist their problem. Thus, there are several matters outstanding
which can be decided only by the Jewish community itself.

Meantime, the children are safe, and are being well cared for. Many
are still in the homes of their foster-parents, some of whom are loath to
give them up, a matter which will require tact and patience for its solution

150

H. W. Emerson
Director

Additional Comment: In a later report dated 8 January 1945, Sir Herbert
Emerson states that the French Government has indicated its interest in
establishing "a system of State guardianship and State care for all children
who have lost their parents, including those within the mandate of the
Intergovernmental Committee. Pending the introduction of that system, the
children are being maintained from voluntary sources. Fourteen homes have
already been opened, and others are in contemplation.. The rest of the
children are still with foster parents. A few of the children who were
given asylum in Switzerland have returned, and a considerable number are
likely to return in the near future."

OFFICE OF CHIEF OF COUNSEL
FOR WAR CRIMES
APO 696-A   U.S. ARMY

STAFF EVIDENCE ANALYSIS, Ministries Division.

By: Mark Schafer.
Date: 15 May 1947.

Document number: NG-1792.

Title and/or general nature: Telegram by BECKERLE regarding
                               his interview with the Premier
                               of Bulgaria, in which he tried
                               to prevent the Bulgarian govern-
                               ment from allowing the transport
                               of 5,000 Jewish children to
                               Palestine.

Form of Document: Mimeographed copy of telegram.

Stamps and other endorsement: Seal of the Foreign Office.

Date: 4 February 1943.

Source: Inl. II g Judenausreise nach
                               Palestina 436777,
                               now at: FO-SD, Building 32 MDB,
                               Berlin,
                               (OCC BBT 1940).

Doc. 13

151

PERSONS OR ORGANIZATIONS IMPLICATED:

                               BECKERLE
                               RITTER
                               ALBRECHT
                               WIEHL
                               SCHMIDT (Paul)
                               WOERMANN.

TO BE FILED UNDER THESE REFERENCE HEADING:

                               NG-Foreign Office
                               NG-Racial and Political Persecution
                               NG-Atrocities.

SUMMARY:

    BECKERLE reports that the Prime Minister of Bulgaria
had told him that the Swiss protective power wanted them to
allow the transfer of 5000 Jewish children to Palestine by
way of Bulgaria. Since BECKERLE was without instructions from
the Foreign Office, he did not know exactly what to say, but
told the Premier that Germany has had bad experiences in the past
by allowing the emigration of Jews, since these are invariably
used abroad for hostile propaganda against Germany.

                Distribution: RITTER
                              ALBRECHT
                              WOERMANN
                              SCHMIDT (of the press)
                              WIEHL.

-- END --

Telegramm
(Geh. Ch. Verf.)

Sofia, den 4. Februar 1943
Ankunft: 5.   "   "   10,08 Uhr

Nr. 176 vom 4. 2.   C i t o !
==

Der Ministerpräsident mitteilte mir bei einem Ge-
spräch, daß über die Schweizer Schutzmacht von englischer
Seite das Angebot gemacht worden sei, etwa 5000 (5000) jüdische
Kinder nach Palästina zu übernehmen. Wenn er auch erklärt,daß
es sich zunächst um eine unverbindliche Anfrage handle, zu der
er noch keinerlei Stellungnahme eingenommen habe, wird er

zweifellos mich zu dieser Frage, sobald
sie offiziell anhängig ist, nach mein +)
hören. Ich bitte daher um Weisung. Ich
habe mich zunächst darauf beschränkt,all-
gemein zu erklären,daß wir schlechte Er -
fahrungen damit gemacht hätten, daß Juden
die Möglichkeit auszuwandern gegeben
wurde, da diese dann im Ausland gegen
uns eingesetzt oder von der feindlichen
Propaganda ausgenutzt worden seien.

+)fehlt
Klartext

152

Beckerle.

Verteiler Nr. 4:

Nr. 1) an D. III   (Arb.2.)
Nr. 1a)
Nr. 2) " RAM
Nr. 2a)
Nr. 3   " St.S.
Nr. 4) " ERAM
Nr. 4a)
Nr. 5   " Botsch. Ritter
Nr. 6-14 " Abt. Leiter:
        6) Pol., 7) Recht,
        8) Dtschld., 9) Ha.Pol,
        10) Kult, 11) Presse,
        12 P.ot., 13) Ru., 14) Inf.
Nr. 15   " Dg. Pol.
Nr. 16   " Dg. Arb. Abt. (wenn nicht Pol Arb.
                Abt. ist)
Nr. 17   " Sammlg. Telko.

Das ist Nr. _____

133782

OFFICE OF CHIEF OF COUNSEL
FOR WAR CRIMES
APO 696-A   U.S.ARMY

STAFF EVIDENCE ANALYSIS, Ministries Division.

By: Mark Schafer
Date: 15 May 1947

Document Number: NG - 1782

Title and/or general nature: Telegram signed by RADEMACHER, stating that the transport of Jewish children from Roumania to Palestine by way of Bulgaria and Turkey must be obstructed in every possible way.

Form of Document: Teletype

Stamps and other endorsements: Signed by RADEMACHER. Initials of PAUSCH

Date: 12 March 1943

Source: Inl. IIg Judenausreise nach Palestine 436777
now at: FOSD, Bldg. 32 MDB, Berlin
(OCC BBT 1937)

Doc. 14

153

PERSONS OR ORGANIZATIONS IMPLICATED:
RADEMACHER
PAUSCH

TO BE FILED UNDER THESE REFERENCE HEADINGS:
NG - Foreign Office
NG - Political and Racial
Persecution
NG - Atrocities

SUMMARY:
Telegram to the German ambassador VON KILLINGER in Sofia:

RADEMACHER states that he has ascertained from press reports that several transports of Jewish children will leave for Palestine from Roumania by way of Bulgaria and Turkey. The transports have been approved by the British.

RADEMACHER is asking that "every possible obstacle" be put in the way of these transports by the German authorities in Roumania and Bulgaria.

E N D

Fernschreiben (G.-Schreiber)

Berlin, den 19 März 1943.

Telegramm { Nicht geh. Ch.V. Offen
           { IZ. (geh. Ch.V.)

Diplogerma
Consugerma Sofia

Geh. Verm. für Behördenleiter
· · · · Geh. Reichssachen
· · · · Geheimsachen
Ohne besonderen Geheimvermerk

Nicht Zutreffendes durch streichen

Nr. _____

Referent: LR Rademacher
         Konsul Pausch.

Betreff: ....
....
....

154

Pressemeldung aus Antyka zu folge seien
im Lager von Athlit in Palästina wieder 72
jüdische Kinder aus Ungarn angekommen, die über
Rumänien, Bulgarien und die Türkei von den
Engländern dorthin befördert worden seien. Dies
sei ein Teil der im Englischen Unterhaus an-
gekündigten Transporte von 270 jüdischen Kindern aus Ungarn und Rumänien. Nach Meldung
palästinischer Presse solle diese Zahl nun auf
500 erhöht werden.

Ausserdem berichtet Gesandtschaft Bukarest
dass in einigen Tagen mit Auswanderung eines
Kontingents jüdischer Kinder aus Rumänien über
Bulgarien und die Türkei auf dem Landwege nach
Palästina begonnen werde. Palästinaamt in
Istanbul habe eine weitere Einreisequote von
etwa 1 000 jüdischen Kindern aus Rumänien
und Transnistrien in Aussicht gestellt. Schliesslich sollen in den nächsten Tagen 150 jüdische Kinder

Freilassen für die Telegramm Kontrolle

277

NG-1712

der aus Rumänien über Bulgarien nach Palästina aus-
wandern.

Bitte der Durchreise dieser Judentransporte
jeden möglichen Widerstand entgegen zu setzen
und über das Ergebnis der Vorstellungen zu berichten.

Bergmann.

NO 2066

File No. 60 D III c 3209

FOLLOW CLOSELY!

1) Use typewriter only
2) Write on one side only
3) Submit open text in special message

4) Telegrams addressed to several addressees may only be transmitted together if they confirm verbally, if slightest variations or additions occur transmit individual telegrams.

Teletype (Secret)

Berlin, 11 March 1943

Telegram: Not secret, open (crossed out)
IX (Secret Ch. V.)

DIPLOGERMA
CONSUGERMA (Crossed out)
No.

(Cross out if not applicable)

Classification Secret for Office Chiefs
            "   "   "   Top Secret Matters
            "   "   "   Secret Matters
Without special (secret) classification

ATTENTION: Legationsrat Rademacher
           Legationssekretaer von Hahn

Doc. 15

156

Referring to written order B III 222g

dated 23 February 1943 —.

Legation Sofia informs, they have gained impression, Bulgarian Government not clearly rejecting inquiry of Protective Power regarding exit of 4000 Jews to Palestine. The assumption therefore seems justified that second part of Stanley's statement dated 3 February (see D III 141 g II dated 13 February) is correct that "previous arrangements have been made to ship 270 Jewish children from Rumania and Hungary to Palestine".

Inland II 925g
Reminder

It is therefore again requested to find out whether negotiations with foreign governments are being carried out or were carried out there regarding the emigration of Jews. Should this be the case the government should be informed at once that emigration of Jews from countries allied with Germany can not be approved by German Government,

leave space for
censor

- 1 -

and that negotiations to that effect are not desired.

Reasons: The fact alone that negotiations concerning the emigration of Jews are carried on makes it possible that 1) our common policy on this important question does not coincide, 2) that separate negotiations might also be successful in other questions, 3) in any case negotiations supply the enemy with propaganda material, 4) agreements about emigration undesired because emigration creates danger of transmitting military information, 5) agreements are contrary to foreign policy towards Arabic Nations. — The German government therefore finds it necessary to request exact information regarding negotiations carried on to date, report on present stage of negotiations, and to ask for the discontinuation of negotiations.

157

(marginal note)

"Wrong of course! This additional note was intended for Rome, merely dictated by me and probably wrongly typed up"

Draft by v. Hahne (illegible initial)

(initials)

- 2 -

OFFICE OF CHIEF OF COUNSEL
FOR WAR CRIMES
APO 696-A   U.S.ARMY

STAFF EVIDENCE ANALYSIS, Ministries Division.

By: Mark Schafer.
Date: 15 May 1947.

Document Number: NG-1805.

Title and/or general nature: Secret telegram by WAGNER,
                                    scorning the Bulgarian govern-
                                    ment for permitting 77 Jewish
                                    children to get through
                                    to Palestine.

Form of Document: Copy of telegram.

Stamps and other endorsements: Signed WAGNER, initialed by
                                    RADEMACHER, THADDEN,
                                    Konsul PAUSCH.

Date: April 1943.

Source: Inl. IIg Judenausreise nach
                                    Palestina 436777,
                                    now at: FO-SD, Building 32
                                    MDB, Berlin,
                                    (OCC BBT 1939).

Doc. 16

158   PERSONS OR ORGANIZATIONS IMPLICATED:

                                    WAGNER, Horst
                                    THADDEN
                                    RADEMACHER
                                    PAUSCH.

TO BE FILED UNDER THESE REFERENCE HEADINGS:

                                    NG-Foreign Office
                                    NG-Persecution of Jews
                                    NG-Atrocities.

SUMMARY:

    WAGNER reports that 77 Jewish children from Roumania have
managed to get to Palestine by way of Bulgaria. The Bulgarian
visa was given to the children on instructions from Sofia.

    "Since the Bulgarian government has thereby acted contrary
to the promises made to us, I asked for explanation and report."

- END -

Akt. Z.

Genau beachten. D III 441 g

1. Nur *Maschinenschrift*
2. Nur *einseitig beschreiben*
3. *Offene* Textteile in besonderem Telegramm absenden

4. Telegramme, die an *mehrere* Anschriften gehen sollen, dürfen nur dann in einer Vfg. erledigt werden, wenn sie *genau wörtlich* übereinstimmen, bei der geringsten Abweichung oder bei Zusätzen ist besonderes Telegramm erforderlich

Drahterlaß

Geheim

Berlin, den .... 19.. 3
         April

Diplogerma
Consugerma
xxxxxxxxxxxxxxNr. S o f i a

Referent: ....
         LR Wagner

Betreff: ....

....

....

Nach Abgang
Pol IV s.g.

2.Wv.: 15.4.

Vermerk:
Paraphe wird wegen Abwesenheit von LR Wagner
nachgeholt.

Freilassen für die Telegramm Kontrolle

Telegramm { Nicht geh. Ch.V. Offen
           (Z. (geh. Ch.V.) xxxxxxx

Geh. Verm. für Behördenleiter
   . . . Geh. Reichssachen
   . . . Geheimsachen
Ohne besonderen Geheimvermerk

Nicht
Zutreffendes
durch
streichen

Unter Bezugnahme auf Drahtbericht
Nr. 399 vom 16.3. und Schriftbericht vom
12.3. - A 313/43 g -.
    Gesandtschaft Bukarest berichtet,
daß Transport jüdischer Kinder in Stärke
von 77 Personen aus Rumänien nach Palästina durch Bulgarien ab Bukarest am 14.3.
bereits durchgereist. Bulgarisches Durch-
reisevisum sei durch Bulgarische Gesandtschaft Bukarest auf Weisung von Sofia
erteilt worden. Da Bulgarische Regierung
somit entgegen uns gegebenen Zusagen ge-
handelt hat, wird um Aufklärung und
Bericht gebeten.
                        W a g n e r

159

Among the most important figures mentioned in the following dossier are:

Erich Albrecht, deputy chief of the legal department in the German foreign ministry

Marschall Jon Antonescu, the prime minister of Rumania

Otto von Erdmannsdorff, deputy chief of the political department of the German foreign ministry. He was acquitted by an American military tribunal in the so-called ministries case.

Peter Anton Feldscher, head of the department of protective power at the Swiss legation in Berlin

Kurt Heinburg, legation counsellor in the political department of the German foreign ministry

Andor Hencke, chief of the political department of the German foreign ministry

Manfred von Killinger, German minister in Budapest

Martin Luther, chief of Department Deutschland, which provided liaison with the SS

Joachim von Ribbentrop, German foreign minister. He was sentenced to death by the International Military Tribunal at Nuernberg and executed there in October 1946.

Gerd Ruehle, chief of the division of political broadcasting in the German foreign ministry

Franz von Sonnleithner, an official in the bureau of the German foreign ministry

Gustav Adolf Steengracht von Moyland, state secretary in the German foreign ministry. He was sentenced to seven years imprisonment by an American military tribunal in the so-called ministries case.

Eberhardt von Thadden, an official in Inland II, which provided liaison with the SS

Horst Wagner, chief of Inland II

STAFF EVIDENCE ANALYSIS, MINISTRIES DIVISION

By: Henry Elias
Date: 20 February 1948

Document number: NG - 5049

Title and/or general nature: Correspondence between
RIBBENTROP, STEENGRACHT,
ERDMANNSDORF, HENCKE, and
others showing their
conspiracy to use the British
proposal to save 5000 Jewish
children, for propaganda
purposes only, without any
intention of accepting this
offer for humanity's sake.

Form of Document: A,B,C,D,E,F,G,H,I,J,K,L,M,N,O
original typescripts, P,Q,R
carboncopies of typescripts,
S and T original typescripts.

Stamps and other endorsements:

A) Signature WAGNER, initials
HENCKE and STEENGRACHT and
v.THADDEN.
B) Signature SONNLEITHNER,
initials of STEENGRACHT,
WAGNER, ERDMANNSDORFF and
HEINBURG.
C) Signature of v.THADDEN,
D) Signature of WAGNER,
initials of a member of
STEENGRACHT'S staff, of
ALBRECHT, HENCKE and
v.THADDEN,
E) Signature of v.THADDEN,
initials of a member of
STEENGRACHT's staff, of
ALBRECHT and HENCKE,
F) Signature of SONNLEITHNER
and of a member of STEEN*
GRACHT's staff,
G) Signature WAGNER, initials
of HENCKE and ERDMANNSDORFF
and v. THADDEN,
H) Signature of HENCKE,
I) initials of von HAEFTEN,
J) Signature RUEHLE,
K) Signature ALBRECHT, initials
of HENCKE and ERDMANNSDORFF
L) Signature WAGNER, initials
of MISBACH (STEENGRACHT's
Staff) and of v. THADDEN,
M) Signature WAGNER
N) Signature WAGNER, initials
STEENGRACHT,
O) Signature WAGNER, initials
of MISBACH (STEENGRACHT's
office) and handwritten
notes and initials of
RIBBENTROP

162

- 1 -

_____

P) Signed WAGNER,
Q) initials of v. THADDEN,
R) None
S) initials of v. THADDEN,
marginal note by
ERDMANNSDORFF in his hand-
writing using his purple
pencil
T) Signature WAGNER.

Date:
A) 7 May 1943
B) 11 May 1943
C) 14 May 1943
D) 21 May 1943
E) 1 June 1943
F) 27 June 1943
G) 25 June 1943
H) 2 July 1943
I) 3 July 1943
J) 10 July 1943
K) 10 July 1943
L) 21 July 1943
M) 12 August 1943
N) 12 October 1943
O) 28 October 1943
P) 6 January 1944
Q) 29 March 1944
R) 27 April 1944
S) 5 May 1944
T) 27 May 1944.

163

Source:
Inl. II g Paket 58/5 FELDSCHER
Aktion (Austausch juedischer
Kinder) now at: FO-SD-
Building E, Mc Nair Barracks,
Berlin
OCC BBT 5363 -T

PERSONS OR ORGANIZATIONS IMPLICATED:

STEENGRACHT
ERDMANNSDORFF
WAGNER
V. THADDEN
HENCKE

TO BE FILED UNDER THESE REFERENCE HEADINGS:

NG - Foreign Office
NG - Racial Persecution

SUMMARY:
A) WAGNER reports to HENCKE, STEENGRACHT and
RIBBENTROP that Rumania wants to let 70,000 Jewish
children leave for Palestine. As this is contrary to
the German policy regarding Jews and Arabs, he suggests
that KILLINGER, the German Ambassador in Bucharest, should
tell ANTONESCU that Germany has promised only to consider
the case, but has not given its approval. Then, as
WAGNER suggests, nothing further should be done unless
Rumania makes a new move.

B) RIBBENTROP orders STEENGRACHT to talk it over with
HIMMLER who should give his view as far as the Jewish question
is concerned, while RIBBENTROP himself will make the political
decision.

C) VON THADDEN informs WAGNER of HIMMLER's stand submitted
by EICHMANN. Emigration of Jewish children has to be
declined. If, however, an exception should be made, four
German internees should be requested in exchange for every
Jewish child. Moreover it is pointed out by EICHMANN that
the negotiations should be speeded up, " as the time is
nearing when the departure of 5000 Jewish children will
become technically impossible, because of the progress of
our Jewish measures."

D) WAGNER reports to ALBRECHT, HENCKE, STEENGRACHT and
RIBBENTROP on the Swiss proposal to take 5000 Jewish children
from the East. At the same time Britain would like to know
Germany's point of view with regard to the emigration of
Jewish children from Germany, Denmark, Belgium, Holland,
Greece and Serbia. This suggestion is along the same lines
as Rumania's re 7000 (not 70.000) Jewish children, and
Bulgaria's promise with regard to her Jewish children.
Bulgaria did not dare to refuse for humanitarian reasons, but
has informed Germany that she will make the departure
impossible in order to fullfill German wishes. Then he
reiterates the point of view expressed by HIMMLER (document C),
by the legal department and by dept. Inl. II.

E) VON THADDEN reports to STEENGRACHT, HENCKE, ALBRECHT
and RIBBENTROP on the new situation which developed from the
offer of the Red Cross to furnish ships for the emigration
of Jewish children from Rumania. Although ANTONESCU accepted
the offer, von THADDEN suggests that KILLINGER should be
ordered to prevent this emigration and to repeat to the
Rumanian government that Germany offers to take the unwanted
Jews off her hands and to deport them to the East to work
there. (Analyst's note: children!) (identical with document
.. of BBT 5218/NG 3987)

F) RIBBENTROP wants STEENGRACHT and WAGNER to examine the
question of emigration of Jewish children in toto and to
suggest future action with regard to emigration to the
Argentine, England, and from German occupied territories.

G) Memo by WAGNER and v. THADDEN to the other departments
of the Foreign Office, advising them of the present state
of the emigration question, offering his suggestion for a
reply and asking for their point of view. WAGNER notes that
RIBBENTROP wants to use this question for propaganda purposes
on the largest scale, as showing Germany's pro-Arabic politics
and England as Philo-semitic.

H) HENCKE who is in charge of the political dept. approves
WAGNER's proposal (doc.G) and suggests that Germany's
satellite states, Rumania, Bulgaria and France should be
informed of the German plan in order to make them go along,
but not of the plan to use it for propaganda, so as to
assure secrecy.

I) Von HAEFTEN, in charge of the dept. for political
culture, concurs too, but suggests that the words "according
to the democratic parliamentarian usage" be struck out, as it
would reveal too clearly the intention to make use of the
affair for propaganda.

164

J) Envoy RUEHLE, gives warning, as chief of his dept., of enemy propaganda which might construe the German stand as a "brutal blackmail attempt or a cynical maneuver in order to gain a carte blanche for future actions against Jews in the German orbit. He too, approves the proposal.

K) ERDMANNSDORFF's, HENCKE's and ALBRECHT's (the latter in charge of the legal dept.) objection/on the unacceptable condition to force the British parliament to adopt the emigration project by a vote, because they fear that the propagandistic effect of the German answer might suffer.

L) WAGNER's report for submission to STEENGRACHT and RIBBENTROP states the different rescue proposals and suggests the official answer. Publication has to wait until the British had answered, but HIMMLER should be asked to stop sending possible subjects of barter to the East, in case England should accept the conditions.

M) Memo by THADDEN and WAGNER noting a change suggested by HIMMLER to increase the propagandistic value of the German answer.

N) WAGNER and STEENGRACHT are asking RIBBENTROP for a quick decision in the emigration question as there are signs that Bulgaria and Rumania are going to act independently.
O) New report by WAGNER and STEENGRACHT to RIBBENTROP asking him to approve the contemplated answer and actions which were agreed to in a conference in STEENGRACHT's office. (Analyst's note: It can be deducted from RIBBENTROP's handwritten notes, that he approved.)

P) WAGNER informs HIMMLER through his adjutant GROTHMANN that RIBBENTROP approved the answer to be given to FELDSCHER, enclosing the text of this answer.

Q) VON THADDEN reports to STEENGRACHT and RIBBENTROP that the above-mentioned German note was answered by England. The Jewish children are to proceed to England, an exchange is out of question as such an exchange could take place only if British subjects were to be matched against German subjects. He suggests that this answer be considered as a rejection of the German suggestions and that a start be made with the publishing of the notes.

R) Detailed proposals of WAGNER's dept. (Probably by him or v. THADDEN) as to the use of the whole FELDSCHER-action for propaganda purposes.

S) Report by v. THADDEN, WAGNER and ERDMANNSDORFF to STEENGRACHT and RIBBENTROP on a new move by FELDSCHER, who promised in the name of England that the Jewish children would be taken to a part of the British Empire, but not to Palestine or the Near East. THADDEN notes that this does not correspond with the German interest which would like to see the children taken to England in order to foster antisemitism there. He mentions that he heard confidentially from the Reichssicherheitshauptamt that 5000 Jewish children were available now only in Litzmannstadt (Lodz), but that this Ghetto also would be dissolved soon. He urges RIBBENTROP's decision.

165

- 4 -

T) Memo by WAGNER to von THADDEN (distribution to STEENGRACHT and HENCKE) stating that RIBBENTROP wants to delay decisions in this matter until the next move of the British.

(Analyst's note: As can be seen also from Documents F and G in BBT 1950, NG 1794, nothing was done to carry out the British proposal, probably, because there were no more Jewish children available.

As Mr. SCHAFER's file, of BBT 1950, did not contain originals with endorsements, comments, etc. it is suggested that the present SEA provides more valuable evidence on the whole incident.)

166

- 5 -
END

to Inl II 1116 secret

Stamp: secret

Note.

Under telegram No. 2370, dated 30 April, Minister von KILLINGER requested definite decision regarding the emigration of 70000 Jewish children up to the age of 8 from Roumania to Palestine. It is understood that Marshal ANTONESCU had been told at the Fuehrer Headquarters that Germany agreed in principle to this emigration.

Although, according to information available at Inl II, the emigration of Jewish children had been discussed between Reich Foreign Minister and Marshal ANTONESCU, the Reich Foreign Minister only promised to examine this question without committing himself to any specific promise.

Group Inl. II holds that the granting of exit permits for 70000 Jewish children would be in contrast to the policy strictly adhered to until now to permit no Jews to emigrate to enemy States from territory under German control or under the control of her Allies. Approval would therefore be considered a change in our basic attitude.

The Pol. Dept. furthermore considers

via Under State Secretary Political Division and

State Secretary

for submission

to the Reich Foreign Minister

initialed: HENCKE 8/5

STEENGRACHT 8/5

- 1 -

167

(page 2 of original)

it objectionable in view of our Arabian policy, to give express per-

mission for the admission of 70,000 Jewish children to Palestine.

Group Inl. II therefore suggests:

1.) The Reich Foreign Minister should instruct Minister von

KILLINGER to point out to the Marshal in a suitable form that

it is merely intended to investigate whether the emigration

of 70,000 Jewish children to Palestine could be approved.

Fundamental approval was by no means granted in the conferences.

A telegram draft to this effect is enclosed:

168

(page 2 of original, cont'd.)

2.) Group Inl. II should instruct the Bucharest Legation,
following the Reich Foreign Minister's telegram, to inform
the Rumanian government delegate LECCA that the investigation
of whether 70,000 Jewish children can be allowed to emigrate
has not yet been concluded. A draft of the proposed telegram
is also enclosed.

3.) Then we should leave the next move to the Rumanians.

Berlin, 7 May 1943

signature: WAGNER
(page 3 of original)   Initial: Thadden
Office of Reich Foreign Minister   Ref. Inl II 1116 g

169

Submitted via State Secretary

Initial: (STEENGRACHT) 12/5

LR WAGNER
                            Stamp: Secret
Initial: (WAGNER) 12/5

Deputy Chief   The Reich Foreign Minister asks you to
Political Division
please consult   confer again with the Reichsfuehrer SS in the

Initial: HENCKE   question of the deportation of 70,000 Jewish
23/5
                            children from Rumania to Palestine, ex-

                            clusively from the point of view of dealing

                            with the Jewish question. The Reich Foreign

                            Minister of course reserves for himself

                            decisions on the political aspect.

Initial:
12/5 HEINBURG   Fuschl, 11 May 1943
To
Minister HEINBURG   Signature
as agreed
                                SONNLEITHNER
Initial: ERDMANNSDORFF 23/5

- 2 -

(page 4 of original)   (Handwritten)

Ref.: Legation Counsellor von THADDEN   Ref. Inl II 1259 g

Secret

SS Obersturmbannfuehrer EICHMANN - Amt IV, Reich Security Main Office - reports that his organization has the following opinion on the Allied wish to evacuate Jewish children from Rumania and the occupied Eastern territories:

1.) The emigration of Jewish children must be opposed on principle.

2.) The emigration of 5,000 Jewish children from the occupied Eastern territories would be approved if they could be exchanged for Germans interned abroad at a rate of 4 to 1, i.e. a total of 20,000 allowed to return to the Reich. It must be emphasized, however, that we want not 20,000 old people, but Germans capable of reproduction, under 40.

Besides, the negotiations must be concluded quickly, since the time is approaching when, as a result of our Jewish measures, the emigration of 5,000 Jewish children from the Eastern territories will be technically impossible.

3.) Insofar as the emigration of Jewish children from Rumania or other Balkan states has to be approved in spite of paragraph 1, this must not be done without some return, but in a process according to paragraph 2.

When I asked whether this position was final and could be submitted to the Reich Foreign Minister as the attitude of the Reichsfuehrer SS, EICHMANN said yes.

To the Head of Group Inland II for his information and with the request for instruction as to whether a final report on the whole matter may now be made to the Reich Foreign Minister.

(Handwritten)   Berlin, 14 May 1943
Inl II 1369 g   Signature: von THADDEN

- 3 -

(page 5 of original)

Ref. Inl. II 1369/43 g

Notes

(Only individual
words legible:)
Submit only
if England ..
pro-Jewish
Arabs

(handwritten
in RIBBENTROP's
handwriting)
Answer
friendly (?)

Minister FELDSCHER Head of Department "Protective
Power" in the Swiss Legation here, submitted to the
Head of the Legal Department, Minister ALBRECHT,
the wish of the British Government that the Germans
might agree to the emigration of 5,000 non-Aryan persons - 85% children and 15% adults for supervision -
from Poland, Lithuania, and Latvia to Palestine.
The British also want to be informed of the Reich
Government's attitude on the emigration of Jewish
children from Germany, Denmark, and the occupied
territories of Holland, Belgium, Greece, and Serbia.

Minister FELDSCHER on this occasion said that
these were persons over whom Switzerland is not
empowered to exercise protection. He therefore
believed

Via

Head of Legal Department

Minister ALBRECHT

Under State Secretary Political Division

to the State Secretary   Initial: 21/5 ALBRECHT

for submission   Initial: HENCKE 22/5

to the Reich Foreign Minister   Initial: MIRBACH 24/5

171

- 4 -

(page 6 of original)

that the inquiry should not be put in the form of a note. When asked whether and what return the British proposed to make, Mr. FELDSCHER said that he had no instructions on that.

This step of the British government is on the same level as the inquiry made at the Rumanian government for approval of the emigration of 7,000 – not 70,000, as assumed because of an error in the telegraphic report – and at the Bulgarian government for 4,000 children and 500 accompanying persons, and is obviously part

of the plan reported in the press to allow 30,000 to 50,000 Jewish children to immigrate to Palestine, thus saving them from the extermination with which they are allegedly threatened.

172

(page 6 of original, cont'd.)

The Bulgarian government has already formally approved the
emigration of Jewish children, since refusal seemed impossible
for humanitarian reasons. It informed the German Legation, however,
that it intended to comply with the German wish that Jewish
emigration be prevented and to allow the emigration to be frustrated
by technical difficulties.

The Rumanian government - as the enclosed correspondence shows-
has not yet answered the inquiry, but has

(page 7 of original)

consulted Berlin via the German Legation in Bucharest, pointing
out that Marshal ANTONESCU when he was at the Fuehrer's Headquarters received the promise of German approval of the exit
permits.   Actually, however, the Reich Foreign Minister merely
promised the Marshal that the matter would be investigated.

With respect to the emigration of Rumanian Jews, the Reich Foreign
Minister has ordered that first of all the Reichsfuehrer SS is to
be consulted. Because of the steps meanwhile taken by Switzerland,
the inquiry was immediately extended to this, too.

The Reichsfuehrer SS stated that for basic considerations we
cannot agree to the emigration of Jewish children from the German
sphere of power and from friendly states. He considers that he might
change his views with respect to emigration from the German sphere only
if, in return for the release of Jewish children for emigration from
the German sphere, young interned Germans be permitted to return
to Germany, on a scale yet to be determined. As a scale the Reichsfuehrer SS suggests one Jew for four Germans.

- 5 -

173

(page 8 of original)

The Legal Department would be very glad if the British

inquiry could be used to resume discussions about returning

interned Germans from Palestine and Australia to Germany, to

arrange for safe conduct for the return of Germans from neutral

territories (Portuguese colonies, Argentina, etc.) and perhaps
                    ethnic and
to arrange for Reich Germans to return home from Paraguay and

Uruguay.

174

(page 8 of original, cont'd.)

Group Inland II actually holds the view that for basic considerations, in agreement with the Reichsfuehrer SS, the emigration of Jewish children from Germany and friendly countries is out of the question. In view of our Arab policy alone, approval to the transfer of Jewish children to Palestine cannot be given. In this connection it is mentioned that the Grand Mufti has submitted a formal protest to the Reich Government and the Italian Embassy here because of the proposed emigration of Bulgarian Jewish children to Palestine, pointing out the danger to vital Arab interests in such immigration.

Group Inland II, however, suggests - in order to get important German forces from abroad and if necessary to make the opponents responsible for the failure of the emigration project for Jewish children - that the British inquiry

(page 9 of original)

answered by a counter inquiry as to whether the British Government is prepared to allow interned Germans to return home under safe conduct, in exchange for the Jewish children. The scale to be suggested here would have to be agreed upon with domestic agencies. If there are exchange negotiations, we should have to consider whether, in the interest of our Arab policy, we should not, at least formally, express the wish that the emigrating Jewish children be sent not to Palestine but elsewhere.

Group Inland II considers it desirable that the British inquiry be answered similarly by all the Tripartite-Pact states to which it is addressed or may yet be addressed. Nor can it be expected that the Rumanian and Bulgarian governments prevent the

175

(page 9 of original, cont'd.)

emigration of Jewish children if the Reich government agrees to an exchange.

Group Inland II therefore suggests that the Bulgarian and Rumanian governments be urged to conform with the German procedure in answering the British inquiry.

Minister BECKERLE considers such a suggestion to the Bulgarian government possible. Since there is no possibility of exchange for the Bulgarians, however, he believes that it is possible to represent the exchange as a pan-European

176

(page 10 of original)

project, so that we might demand the release of interned Germans in return for the Bulgarian Jewish children, as well.

The Rumanian government should also be informed, when our wishes are presented, that when Marshal ANTONESCU was at the Fuehrer's Headquarters the Reich Foreign Minister did not promise him unconditional approval of permission to emigrate, but only that the English request would be investigated.

Berlin, 21 May 1943

Signature: WAGNER

(page 11 of original)

172   Inland II 231 g R 1 first copy   **177**

Inl. II   Stamp: Secret Reich Matter

Note for oral report.

In the note for oral report of 21 May 1943 - Inland II 1369 g - instructions were requested from the Reich Foreign Minister about further treatment of the proposed emigration of Jewish children from Rumania, Bulgaria, and the occupied Eastern territories.

Minister von KILLINGER on 27/5 reported by wire that representatives of the International Red Cross asked Marshal ANTONESCU whether the Rumanian government would support the emigration of Jews from Transnistria on Red Cross ships. The Marshal, who disapproves of the concentration of Jews in Transnistria and who absolutely wants to get rid of the Jews, replied that it would be a new situation for him if the emigration were to be not in Rumanian ships, but in ships supplied by the Red Cross.

(page 11 of original, cont'd.)

Minister von KILLINGER asked for wire instructions on the Reich Government's position in this question.

Inland II suggests that Minister von KILLINGER be instructed to urge the Rumanian government

Via

Head of Legal Department	initialed ALBRECHT 3/6
Under State Secretary Political Division	" HENCKE 7/6
to the State Secretary	" MIRBACH 10/6

submitted to the Reich Foreign Minister

178

(page 12 of original)

to prevent the emigration of Jews from Rumania, even if the International Red Cross supplies the necessary shipping space.

On this occasion the willingness of the Reich Government to take the unwanted Jews off the Rumanian government's hands and put them to work in the East should again be expressed.

Berlin, 1 June 1943

(On instructions of Head of Group Inland II)

by order

Signature: von THADDEN

Legation Counsellor

(page 13 of original)

179

Office of Reich Foreign Minister

Via State Secretary

has been submitted to State Secretary Initial: MIRBACH

Legation Counsellor WAGNER.

The Reich Foreign Minister asks you to investigate the question of immigration of Jewish children to Argentina together with the other pending questions on the emigration of Jews from our sphere of power and to make a suggestion to the Reich Foreign Minister about the further handling of the question.

The Reich Foreign Minister recalls especially that the British approached us about the emigration of Jews.

Fuschl, 27 June 1943   SONNLEITHNER

(handwritten·) SONNLEITHNER

unknown initials 28/6

- 8 -

(page 14 of original)

Ref. Legation Counsellor von THADDEN   Inland II 1825 g I

Secret

Notes.

Dirigent)taken   Minister FELDSCHER, Head of the Department
Political)care
Division) of   Protective Power in the Swiss Legation here,
please   )
consult)   was empowered to inquire of the Foreign
HENCKE :Initial)
1 VII   )   Office on behalf of the British government

whether the Germans were willing to agree to

the emigration of 5,000 non-Aryan persons from

Poland, Lithuania, and Latvia, predominantly

children, to Palestine.

180

(page 14 of original, cont'd.)

The details of this as well as of the similar requests to
other governments can be seen from the notes of 21 May, a copy
of which is attached. In addition, the French Embassy in Ankara –
it is not known at whose suggestion – submitted to the government
in Vichy the question of whether exit permits or transit visas
should be given to 2,000 Jewish children from France, 500 from
Holland, 500 from Belgium, and a few hundred from Switzerland,
who were to travel via Lisbon. The French Foreign Ministry asked
the German Embassy in Paris what the position of the Reich Government is in this matter.

The Reich Foreign Minister and the Reichsfuehrer SS have decided
that the inquiry of Minister FELDSCHER to the Reich Government is
to be answered to the effect that there is willingness to negotiate
if the English government is prepared to take the Jews into
England instead of Palestine and has this willingness sanctioned
by a resolution of the House. of Commons. /The Reich Foreign Minister
has also ordered that the matter is to be exploited as much as
possible for propaganda purposes, both as proof of our pro-Arab
attitude in the Palestine question and as evidence of the pro-
Jewish attitude of the English.

(page 15 of original)

It is to be expected that the British will not accept the
demand. In this case the responsibility clearly lies with the
English. If, contrary to expectation, England should comply with
our request, this will be especially good for propaganda use and
should also give us the opportunity to suggest the exchange of the
Jews for interned Germans.

- 9 -

181

(page 15 of original, cont'd.)

Inland II intends to give the following answer to the Swiss
Legation (in the same form as the inquiry):

"Although the request of the British government for exit

permit   for 5,000 Jews does not reveal whether the British

are willing to make any concessions in return, perhaps an

exchange of the Jews for internees, the Reich Government is

prepared to comply with the British request.

Since, however, in the view of the Reich Government, Palestine

is in the Arabian Lebensraum, negotiations for the emigration

of the Jews could be entered into only on condition that the

British government agrees that the Jews be sent to England

instead of Palestine and has this intention sanctioned -

according to democratic-parliamentary practice - by a

resolution of the British House of Commons.

Berlin,

182

Department Inl. II would be grateful for your immediate comments
in this matter, especially as to whether the suggested wording
of the reply is expedient from the point of view of making use
of the propagandistic possibilities.

Deputy Chief Political Division

F

= Settled.

Furthermore, Inland II requests your comments, especially those
of the Political Department as to whether it would not be advisable
to inform the Rumanian, Bulgarian, and French Government in time
about the German plan, in view of the British inquiry addressed
to them, and to ask the Paris Embassy, and/or the Legations in

(page 16 of original)

183

Sofia and Bukarest, to suggest to them a suitable procedure.

Herewith submitted separately to

Initial:

Under State Secretary Political Division   X HINCKE 1. VII.
Department Chief of Legal Department
    "   "   "   Cultural and political Department

    "   "   "   Press Department
    "   "   "   Radio Department
Official in charge of Information Department

for their comments.

Berlin 25 June 1943

Signature: WAGNER
(page 17 of original)   Initial: von Thadden

Foreign Office

Inland II 1900 g

received 5 July 1943

enclosure (-fold) duplicate of document received.
Secret.

Political Department approves your suggestion regarding the
propagandistic value of the reply to be given to the Swiss Le-

(page 17 of original cont'd)

gation in connection with the emigration of 5,000 Jews from the
East to England, instead of to Palestine.

184

(page 17 of original cont'd)

The Political Department also considers it expedient to inform the Rumanian,
Bulgarian, and French Government in time about the German plan,
in view of the British inquiry addressed to them and to ask our
Missions to suggest to them a suitable procedure. The afore-mentioned
Governments should, however, only be informed about the fact of the
inquiry and the contents of our reply, but for secrecy reasons
they should not be told about our intentions of exploiting the
propaganda value.

    Herewith to

        Department Inland II

With reference to letter of 25 June of this year — Inland II
1825 I

        Berlin, 2 July 1943

          Signature: HENCKE.

Herrn v. THADDEN.

        (page 18 of original)

Cultural Political   (Inland II 1825 secret to Cul-
Division.   tural Political Division 3460 secret).
Legation Councillor von HAEFFEN

It is suggested to cross out the parenthesis "in accordance with
democratic-parlamentary practice" in the draft of a verbal note
to be addressed to the Swiss Legation in connection with the exit
permit for Jews, as this would betray our intentions of utilizing
the matter for propagandistic purposes.

    Handwritten: Herewith again submitted to Legation Councillor

                von THADDEN.

        Initial: HAEFFEN, 3 July.

          - 11 -

185

(page 18 of original cont'd)

Minister RUEHLE   Berlin 10 July 1943

With reference to Inland II   Stamp: Secret

1825 secret V.

The following comments are made with regard to the emigration
of 5000 Jews to Palestine:

The matter must be treated very carefully with regard to the
Information Service abroad. The propaganda offices of our
enemies must not be given any opportunity of making the German
proposal look like a brutal attempt at blackmail, or a cynical
manoeuver by which we were trying to obtain indemnification for
future measures to be taken against the Jews in territories
under German rule. It must be taken into consideration that even
many anti-semites abroad are having considerable misgivings about
the harsh treatment of the Jews.

186

(page 19 of original cont'd)

The reply which "Inland II" intends to send takes these dangers
into consideration. The only thing which might be considered is
whether one should not refrain from insisting in the second paragraph that the Jews be taken to England, but should only demand
that they should not be transferred to Palestine or any other
Arabic territory. Furthermore, it would make a more favorable
impression from the point of view of information abroad if one
would not demand a Resolution by the House of Commons, but
only safe guarantees for the promise of the British Government.

Signature: · RUEHLE

Inland II
Legation Councillor WAGNER

(page 20 of original)

Ref. i. V. Ks SAKOWSKY   to Inland II 1825 g II

187

Immediately
----- ------

The decision regarding the entry into England is a matter
of the Home Office, which makes use of the Immigration Office for
carrying out the regulations in connection with entry permits. As
the 5000 Jews are to be received into England, i.e. not only
allowed to stay there for a limited period, but to take up their
permanent residence, there the British will not only have to
grant them an entry permit, but also the permit for permanent
residence. For the residence permit, too, the Home
Office is competent.

It is difficult to judge whether the British Home Secretary would
decide the matter without being sure of his support. If he were in
doubt he would probably put the matter to the Cabinet.

- 12 -

(page 20 of original cont'd)

A resolution by the House of Commons is out of the question as the
matter does not come within its competency according to English
National Law.

If the German Government in its reply to the British Government
demanded that the Jews' entry into England and their residence
there should be sanctioned by a resolution of the British House
of Commons, the British Government would doubtlessly point out
that the House of Commons is not authorized to deal with the matter,
and that the German Government had made such requests as could not
be complied with according to English National Law, in order to make
the affair fail. In this way the propagandistic effect of the
German reply which the German Government strives to achieve, would
probably be jeopardized.

188

Under State Secretary

Political Division

Deputy Chief   Political Division f =

Initial :   (E) ERDMANNSDORFF 14

Herewith submitted to
Initial:
HENCKE   Inland II
via Pol.
on 15 July

Berlin 10 July 1943

Signature: ALBRECHT

(page 21 of original)

Inland II   Inland II 2092 g
                                  Stamp: Secret

Notes on Report
_____

illegible   As is shown by numerous reports received, the
stenographic
notes.   Action Juive is endeavoring, with the help of the Govern-

              ments of the Enemy States, to get 50,000 Jews out of the

              territories under German rule. The following individual

              actions forming part of this over all operation have up

              to now been brought to the notice of the Foreign Office:

              1. Inquiry addressed on behalf of the British Government

                 by Minister FELDSCHER of the Swiss Legation about

                 the emigration of 5,000 Jewish children from the occu-

                 pied Eastern territories to Palestine.

              2. Inquiry addressed by Minister FELDSCHER as to the

                 Reich Government's fundamental attitude concerning the

                 emigration of Jews from the occupied Western territories.

              3. Inquiry addressed by Switzerland to Sofia on behalf of

                 the British Government, about the emigration of 5,000

                 Bulgarian Jews to Palestine.

              4. Inquiry addressed by the International Red Cross to

                 the German Embassy at Ankara concerning the granting of

                 safe transit for 1,000 Bulgarian Jews from a Bulgarian

                 port to Palestine.

To be submitted   Stamp:

via
                                   Seen by the   State Secretary
the State Secretary to the Reich Foreign Minister
                                           initial: MIREACH

189

(page 21 of original cont'd)

the following Divisions: Political, Legal, Cultural

Political, Press, Radio, B.f.I., Inland I,

Political Division I M

(have received duplicates)

(page 22 of original)

5. Inquiry addressed by the Rumanian Government with a view

to obtaining the Reich Government's permission for 7.000

Rumanian Jews to emigrate to Palestine (according to the
allegedly
Rumanian version this/has already been promised to Marshal

ANTONESCU by the Reich   Foreign Minister)

190

(page 22 of original)

6. Inquiry addressed by the Swedish Legation on behalf of the Dutch Emigrant Government about the emigration of 500 Dutch Jews to Palestine.

7. Inquiry addressed by the French Government as to the Reich Government's attitude with regard to the emigration of 2,000 Jewish children from France, 500 from Holland, 500 from Belgium, and to the transit of several hundreds from Switzerland via Portugal, to Palestine.

8. Steps taken by the Red Cross in connection with the emigration of Slovakian Jews to Palestine (as Slovakia has not been recognized by the enemy powers, no official inquiry has been addressed).

9. Endeavors made in connection with the emigration of individual groups of Hungarian Jews to Palestine (the Hungarian Ministry for Foreign Affairs states that they know nothing of this).

10. Inquiry addressed by the Argentine Government about the emigration of 1.000 Jewish children from the Reich to Argentine. The inquiries addressed by Minister FELDSCHER (mentioned under No. 1 and 2)

(page 23 of original)

have already been made the subject of discussion between the Reich Minister for Foreign Affairs and the Reichsfuehrer SS . On the basis of this discussion the Reich Minister for Foreign Affairs has issued instructions that a possible reply to the Swiss Legation should be examined from the following points of view:

Refusal to grant exit permit to Palestine, as it is Arabian Lebensraum; Readiness to negotiate in case children are taken to Great Britain proper; Condition: that permission to enter England should be sanctioned by a resolution passed by the House

191

- 14 -

(page 23 of original cont'd)

of Commons:

In addition, the Reich Minister for Foreign Affairs has reserved his decision in the matter of the Rumanian inquiry (No. 5) and has issued instructions that a proposition should be submitted to him in connection with the Argentinian inquiry (No. 10).

The comments of the competent divisions of the Foreign Office (Political Division Legal, Cultural Political, Press, Radio, B.f.I, Inland I, Political I M) on the question of an emigration of Jews from Europe, have been obtained in the first instance by an inquiry ч addressed to all departments by Inland II, and further by a final discussion at the office of the Under State Secretary which the Department Chiefs concerned attended.

192

(page 24 of original)

It was unanimously agreed that the individual inquiries which in
spite of their variety are based on a uniform procedure of the
Action Juive, should also be uniformly dealt with.

In connection with the reply to the FELDSCHER inquiries the
joint examination showed that according to British National Law
the House of Commons is not competent to pass a resolution with
regard to the granting of entry permits to Jews. Therefore the
intended request for a sanction by the House of Commons, does
not appear advisable, as it might give the British Government the
possibility of shifting the responsibility for a failure of the
operation on to the Reich Government, on account of their having
made a request which could not be complied with for legal reasons.
Therefore, instead of the approval of the House of Commons one
should demand a resolution passed by the British Cabinet.

In agreement with the Divisions concerned I thus propose the
following and would ask the Reich Minister for Foreign Affairs
to approve it:

I. Reply to the Inquiries:

1. Minister FELDSCHER will be notified as follows, in the same
   form in which he addressed the British inquiry to us:
   "Although the inquiry of the British Government about the
   granting of exit permits to

                  (page 25 of original)

5,000 Jews does not make it clear whether Britain would be
prepared to do something in return, say by exchanging the Jews for
Germans who are prevented from returning to the Reich by war conditions, the Reich Government is on principle prepared to consider

                          - 15 -

193

(page 25 of original cont'd)

the British request from a positive point of view and to enter
into the necessary negotiations.

As, however, in the view of the Reich Government, Palestine forms
a part of Arabic Lebensraum, these negotiations could only be
taken up under the condition that the British Government, on the
basis of a resolution passed by the Cabinet, agrees to the
Jews being transferred to Great Britain instead of to Palestine,
and being granted permission to take up permanent residence there."

194

(page 25 of original cont'd)

2. A corresponding reply will be given to Minister FELDSCHER in
connection with the emigration of Jews from the occupied
Western territories, and to the Swedish Legation to be passed
on to the Dutch Emigrant Government.

3. It will be suggested to the Bulgarian, Rumanian, and French
Governments that they should give corresponding replies to the
British, and in case there are not sufficient Bulgarians,
Rumanians, or Frenchmen available who want to return home, to ex-
tend the exchange to subjects of the Tripartite-Pact-States,
as this is an over-all European operation.

4. The Governments of Italy, Hungary, Croatia, and Slovakia will be
(page 26 of original)
notified of the reply to Minister FELDSCHER, and it will be
suggested to them that in case they receive similar proposals
from the Government of an enemy State or from the International
Red Cross, they should proceed accordingly.

5. The inquiry addressed by the Red Cross as to whether safe
conduct could be granted for transports of Jews from Bulgaria
to Haifa, is answered in the negative, with reference to the German
attitude in connection with the British inquiry.

6. It will be replied to the Argentinian Embassy that the Reich
Government is prepared to consider the granting of exit permits
to 1000 Jewish children emigrating from the Reich to Argentine,
if the Argentinian Government will, in return, make it possible
for 1000 Germans, wishing to come back from South or Central
America, to return to the Reich under safe conduct granted by the
Americans, British, and the other States at war with the Reich.

II. Utilization for propagandistic purposes:

195

- 16 -

(Page 26 of original cont'd)

For the time being the reply ----- to the British Government
will not be published. The matter will be utilized from a
propaganda point of view as soon as it becomes clear which
consequences the British Government is going to draw from the
German attitude.

However, the German reply will be brought to the notice of
the

196

(page 27 of original)

Grand Mufti and other Arabian circles concerned.

III. Preparations in case the British Government makes a positive

decision:

Though one must count on the British Government refusing to

comply with the German demands   the Reichsfuehrer SS should be

asked, as a precautionary measure, that the barter objects which

might under given circumstances be required should not be

evacuated to the Eastern territories for the time being.

Berlin, 21 July 1943

Signature: WAGNER

initial

von THADDEN

21 July

197

(page 28 of original)

Referent: Legation Counsellor v. THADDEN

Handwritten notice
submitted
to be re-submitted   Shorthand notes

on 24 August   To Inland II 2092 secret
                                       Stamp: Secret
(S) SONNLEITHNER

The Reich Foreign Minister ordered the memorandum of Inland
II 2092 secret of 21 July of this year to be re-submitted after a
week. The Ministerial Office has informed us that it will
take care of this date.

Inland II wants to add the following in this matter:

The Reich Fuehrer SS agrees to the suggestions made by Inland
II to the Reich Foreign Minister and approves of the procedure in
the suggested form. He only suggests to make the suggested wording
of the answer to be given to Minister FELDSCHER (compare page 5
of memo) even more effective from the viewpoint of propaganda taking
into consideration the mentality of the Arabs and to replace the
words "as, however, in the view of the Reich Government Palestine
forms a part of the Arabic Lebensraum by "as, however the Reich
government cannot lend itself to let such a noble and gallant
people like the Arabs be pushed out of their native country Palestine,
these negotiations ....." The Reich Fuehrer believes that such stron-
ger wording will if properly utilized from the propagandistic angle,
result in an increased sabotage activity of national Arabic circles
in the Near East.

Inland II has no objections against the suggested changes, since
they do not change the basic contents of the suggested note.

For the rest the situation has not changed in comparison to the
way it was described in the memorandum of 21 July.

26 August   Berlin, 12 August 1943
                                   Signature: WAGNER
                    - 17 -

(page 29 of Original)

To Inland II 2092 secret

Stamp :SECRET

The French Government requested again information concerning the attitude of the Reich Government with regard to the suggestion of the Government of Argentine to take over 1,000 Jewish children.

From special sources ("Brown Friend" - "Brauner Freund") we can see that Rumania, too, intends to follow its own ways with regard to the question of granting exit permits to Jews, if the Reich government does not indicate its position as requested.

There are also more and more signs that Bulgaria will in time grant an exit permit to at least about 1,000 of the 5,000 Jews who have been offered acceptance by enemy countries.

Inland II therefore requests to ask the Reich Foreign Minister to state his opinion with regard to the memoranda of 21 July and 12 August.

Initial:STEENGRACHT 16.10

Herewith submitted to the office of the Reich Foreign Minister via State Secretary

To be re-submitted
in a week

Berlin, 12 October 1943

Signature

WAGNER

unidentified check mark
19.10.

-19-

199

(Page 30 of original)

(Stamp) secret

Inland ll 2964 secret

MEMORANDUM

The head of the department "Protective Power" of the Swiss
Legation here submitted to the Foreign Office the request of the
British Government for German approval to the emigration of
5,000 non-Aryan persons — 65% children and 15% adults
supervising

from Poland, Lithuania and Latvia to Palestine.
Furthermore, the British would be interested to learn about the
position of the Reich Government with regard to the emigration
of Jewish children from Germany, Denmark and the occupied Dutch,
Belgian, Greek and Serbian territories.

After having examined the matter thoroughly in a work
discussion with the State Secretary with all the interested heads
of the departments attending the meeting, and after having secured
the opinion of the Reich Fuehrer SS, Inland II in agreement with
the aforementioned parties suggests to address to the Swiss Legation
along the following lines:
Herewith submitted via the State Secretary
to the office of the Reich Foreign Minister

(Stamp)   Initial: Mirbach
Has been submitted to the State Secretary

"Although the request of the British
government for exit permit   to
5,000 Jews

-20-

200

(Page 31 of original)

(handwritten)

Not Jews against
Germans

does not reveal whether the British
are willing to make concessions in return-
perhaps an exchange of the Jews for Germans
who are prevented from returning to the
Reich through the war situation, the Reich
Government agrees on principle to consider
the British request favorably and to
enter into negotiations concerning this
matter.

201

(handwritten)

King and
House of
Commons

Since, however, the Reich Government cannot
lend itself to let such a noble and gallant
people like the Arabs be pushed out of
Palestine, their native country, by the Jews,
negotiations of this kind could only be initiated
if the British Government pursuant-to-a-cabinet
decision-*) agrees to have the Jews transferred
to Great Britain instead of Palestine and to
grant them permanent residence there."

*) crossed out

The Reich Fuehrer SS believes that even
if the British refuse such a policy will have a favorable influence
on the national Arab circles. Should, contrary to all expectations,
the British accept these conditions we can assume that antisemitism
in Great Britain will receive new impetus not at all wanted by the
Government through the many thousands of Jews to be expected to
immigrate into Great Britain; at the same time there would be a possibility to have, in exchange for the Jews thousands of interned Germans
or other Germans willing to go home to the Reich.

Ia

202

(Page 32 of original)

Since the inquiry of the Swiss Legation constitutes only one
part of the total program of the Action Juive for the salvation of
30,-50,000 Jews from Europe — the Rumanian, Bulgarian and French
Governments have received similar inquiries from the Allies, and the
government

(Page 32 of original, cont'd)

of Argentine has turned to the Reich Government with regard to the
same matter — and since in the near future we will have to count
on increased activities in connection with this question (compare
enclosure No. 7), Inland II requests authorization to give a
suitable answer to the Argentine Government and to suggest to the
Rumanian, Bulgarian and French governments to treat the requests
addressed to them in the same way. More details concerning the
other inquiries can be seen from the enclosures.

Berlin, 28 October 1943

(handwritten)

(handwritten note
by RIBBENTROP:)
Want to see Argentine
first
memorandum
Ja
RIBBENTROP's initial

Signature : WAGNER

203

(Page 33 of original)

Copy as draft

Foreign Office   (final copy l.b.) Jo

No. Inland II 28 secret   (stamp:)
                                        secret
                                                    6 January 1944

                            by courier

(handwritten)

please (?) comrade (?) v. THADDEN

Dear comrade GROTHMANN.

    After having reported to the Reich Foreign Minister the opinion

of the Reich Fuehrer with regard to the Feldscher matter concerning

5,000 Jewish children, the Reich Foreign Minister considered the

attached wording of an answer to be given orally to Minister FELISCHER,

to be the most expedient and he ordered that Minister FELDSCHER is to

be informed along these lines within the next few days.

              May I ask you to inform the Reich Fuehrer accord-
              ingly
                (crossed out) Heil Hitler (handwritten)

                    By order
           Signature: WAGNER (handwritten)

                    signed v. THADDEN

To SS Sturmbannfuehrer GROTHMANN

Office of the Adjutant of the Reich Fuehrer SS

Field Quarters

(Stamp)dispatched: 7 January 1944   (handwritten)

      1 enclosure   Emigration of Jews

(Page 34 of original)

Inland II 28 secret

Answer to be given orally to Minister FELDSCHER with regard to
the British request.

Although the inquiry of the British government about the
granting of exit permits to 5,000 Jews does not make it clear
what the British government prepared to offer in return, the
Reich government is not averse to consider the British request
and to enter into negotiations concerning this matter.

Since, however, the Reich Government cannot lend itself
to let such a noble and gallant people like the Arabs be pushed
out of Palestine, their native country, by the Jews, these
negotiations can be started only on condition that the British
government agrees to take the Jews to Great Britain instead of
Palestine and to guarantee them permanent residence there.

205

(Page 35 of original)

Group Inland II   Inland II B A 1139

MEMORANDUM

On the basis of the attitude of the Reich Government with regard to the granting of exit permits for 5,000 Jewish children to Palestine Minister FELDSCHER condensed the British inquiry as follows:

, "The children are to be taken to England. However, an exchange is out of question, since the British government is of the opinion that Germans can only be exchanged against subjects of the British Empire."

Whether this condensation is to be taken as the only answer to be expected was not stated by Minister FELDSCHER.

The Germans had raised the question about a counter offer without specifically referring to an exchange. This means that the British government refuses an exchange which was not even suggested, without discussing other possibilities for concessions ..... on the other hand request was made

(stamp)

Herewith submitted via the State Secretary to the Reich Foreign Minister (handwritten)

(departments: political division, radio, cultural/political division, press and legal divisions have received copies) dispatched 30 March

-23-

(Page 36 of original)

to grant permanent residence for the Jews in Great Britain. The British only declare their readiness to accept them without making any statements concerning the duration; it must be assumed that the British plan only a temporary acceptance and intend to send them to Palestine later on.

Group Inland II therefore considers the "condensation" as a rejection of the German suggestions which, for tactical reasons was not made in the form of an answer in order to put the blame for the refusal on us and thus make us responsible for the failure of this action.

207

Group Inland II suggests:

1) Minister FELDSCHER will be informed orally:

The Reich Government has taken notice of the condensation of the British attitude and can interpret it only as a rejection of the German suggestions since it does not reveal whether the acceptance in England will be permanent and since it refuses an exchange of non-British persons against Germans.

Incidentally, the Reich Government has not suggested such an exchange but only generally discussed the question of a return offer. Germany considers the Jews

(Page 37 of original)

as asocial elements. Since the British are interested in these asocial elements, the Reich Government could imagine a return offer in the following manner: an exchange of Jews against persons, who are not German nationals, but whom the British consider as asocial, and in whom Germany is interested, namely, Irish nationalists, Indians, Arabs and Egyptians who were arrested in the British sphere of influence.

2) The first British inquiry and the German answer given last January have already been approved by the Reich Foreign Minister and are now being published in a publication similar to the White Book concerning the Palestine question.

3) The British condensation will be published as a rejection. The commentaries will emphasize the following points of view:

Escape into formalism in order to avoid a rejection by actually at the same time avoiding a reception of the Jews in England, of which one is afraid because of the antisemitism at home. — It is obvious that it is intended to send the Jews from England to Palestine and not to treat them

(Page 38 of original)

as equals of the British, i.e. as second class people.

(Page 38 of original, cont'd)

4) There will, for the time being, not be any publication of the
attitude of the Reich government as suggested under 1) in order not to
put a stop to the discussion with the British and in order to take
up the matter again in one or two months for the sake of propaganda.

Berlin, 29 March 1944

(initials) von THADDEN

209

(Page 39 of original)

Group Inland II

MEMORANDUM

After having heard the opinion of the departments and groups of the
Foreign Office concerned, I suggest to inform Minister FELDSCHER
that the condensation of the British inquiry cannot be considered
a positive answer to our attitude. We only can state with regret
that the discussions must be considered as having failed due to the
unsatisfying answer of the British.

Furthermore I suggest to lift the ban on the so-called
FELDSCHER matter and to turn it over to the propagandists for their
utilization.

At the same time I submit the manuscript of a pamphlet prepared
in co-operation with Information Section XIV by the Cultural Political
Department upon suggestion of Inland II;

(Page 40 of original)

it deals with the British White Book on Palestine and the FELDSCHER
matter is incorporated as evidence for Germany's clear policies
with regard to the Jewish question towards the Arabs. The pamphlet
is to be published with a smashing title — the present "Palestine —
test of power between England and Juda" is only a temporary title —
as a publication of the Institute for History of Modern Germany
or of some other anti-Jewish institute and is to be distributed to
the missions abroad via the Cultural Political Division.

Herewith submitted to the Reich Foreign Minister
with the request for his approval

Berlin, 27 April 1944

(page 41 of original)

(handwritten) Arabia committee
underneath: illegible

(handwritten) NEGELE

Group Inland II   Inland II A 574 secret

MEMORANDUM

Handwritten
MEF (apparently: folder Reich Fuehrer)

(handwritten)   On 2 May 1944 Minister FELDSCHER again   211

Where 5000   approached the head of the legal department
children
counter offer   with the matter concerning the emigration of
Jewish
Arabs   5,000 Jewish children and on this occasion he

To the Senior   expressed another condensation of the British
Legation
Counsellor Wagner   point of view to the effect that the British
for his infor-
mation   Government wants to receive these Jewish children
Initials:
von THADDEN 5/5   "within the British Empire outside of Palestine

                     and the Near East". The question for the

                     German government is whether it is ready to

                     give up those Jewish children under these

                     conditions without any compensation.

(Page 41 of original, cont'd)

Germany had demanded a reception in England, in
order, should the matter be settled in a positive way, to promote
antisemitism in England as a result of the immigration of the
Jews.

Confidential

(handwritten) Jews as an exchange to Arabia

The Reich Security Main Office gave confidential information that
the only place where 5,000 Jewish children considered for emigration
can still be found is the Ghetto of Litzmannstadt. However, this
Ghetto will soon be liquidated upon directive of the Reich Fuehrer SS.

Herewith submitted to the office of the Reich
Foreign Minister

via the State Secretary

with the request to inform in due time Inland II of the decision
of the Reich Foreign Minister about the material submitted by the
State Secretary with regard to the FELDSCHER matter.

Berlin, 5 May 1944
(initials) von THADDEN

(Page 42 of original)

Group leader Inland II

The Reich Foreign Minister ordered that at present nothing is to be done in the FELDSCHER matter (British inquiry for exit permits for 5,000 Jewish children). Dr. MEGERLE's material is to be submitted immediately if this matter is again taken up by the British.

Herewith to

Counsellor of the Legation First Class v. THADDEN.

Salzburg, 27 May 1944

213

(handwritten)
Signature: Wagner

✳✳✳✳✳✳✳

Office of the Reich Foreign Minister
State Secretary
Dr. MEGERLE
Under State Secretary Political Division
Department Legal
     separately

CERTIFICATE OF TRANSLATION

10 June 1948

We, Julia KERR, Virginia von SCHON, and Thea von SEUFFERT,
we hereby certify that we are duly appointed translators for the
German and English languages and that the above is a true and
correct translation of the document No. NG-5049.

Julia KERR   Civ. No. ....

Virginia von SCHON Civ. No. ....

Thea v. SEUFFERT   Civ. No. B-397 929   ....

214

OFFICE OF CHIEF OF COUNSEL
FOR WAR CRIMES
APO 696-A   U.S.ARMY

STAFF EVIDENCE ANALYSIS, Ministries Division.

By: Mark Schafer.
Date: 22 May 1947.

Document number: NG-1794.

Title and/or general nature: Notes by VON THADDEN and WAGNER
                                     showing that they were determined
                                     to prevent the evacuation of
                                     5000 Jewish children from
                                     Eastern Europe to either Palestine
                                     or Canada at all costs.

Form of Document: Original typescripts.

Stamps and other endorsements: A) Signature of VON THADDEN
                                B) Initials of VON THADDEN
                                D) Initials of VON THADDEN
                                E) Signature of MEGERLE.

Date: 8 February 1944 to 12 May 1944.   *Doc. 18*

Source: Inland II A/B Auswaertiges Amt.
                                    Geschaeftszeichen 83-24A."Gruen-   215
                                    dung eines Palaestina-Staates."
                                    Now at: FO-SD, Building 32,
                                    MCB, Berlin,
                                    (OCC BBT 1980 A-G).

PERSONS OR ORGANIZATIONS IMPLICATED:

                                    VON THADDEN
                                    HORST WAGNER
                                    SONNLEITHNER
                                    Dr.MEGERLE
                                    KUTSCHER
                                    COLIN ROSS
                                    SS-Sturmbannfuehrer GUENTHER
                                    Ambassador FELDSCHER
                                    SS-Obersturmfuehrer EICHMANN
                                    STEENGRACHT.

TO BE FILED UNDER THESE REFERENCE HEADINGS:

                                    NG-Foreign Office
                                    NG-Persecution of Jews
                                    NG-Atrocities
                                        (See S.E.A. BBT 1940).

:.

SUMMARY:

A - Note, signed by VON THADDEN, states that he has forwarded
the matter regarding the 5000 Jewish children through
Dr.MEGERLE to VON SONNLEITHNER with the remark that he
has discussed it with COLIN ROSS. The latter is said to have
apologized for the nature of his letter to RIBBENTROP
which allegedly was written in ignorance of the full facts
of this matter. ROSS promised that he would now withdraw
his letter.

B - Second note by VON THADDEN refers to an interview with SS-
Sturmbannfuehrer GUENTHER, which reveals that Ambassador
FELDSCHER, director of the Protective Power with the
Swiss embassy, has received word from the British government that Great Britain is now prepared to accept the
5000 children into the British Empire outside Palestine or
the near East. FELDSCHER would like to know whether Germany
will release the children. VON THADDEN states that the
question regarding the release of the children "is being
further examined by the Foreign Office. "Note was transmitted to EICHMANN and the RSHA. (Reich Central Security
Office).

216

C - Note (by VON THADDEN?), states that ambassador FELDSCHER
should be told that the fact that England is prepared to
accept the children herself could not be considered as
a satisfactory answer to Germany and that the negotiations
as a failure. The note further proposes that now the
material relative to this case should be released for
propagandistic exploitation".

D - Note by v.THADDEN reveals that the British government had
contacted the Swiss legation with regard to that evacuation
of 5000 "non-Aryans", 85% children and 15% adults to
accompany the children, from Poland, Latvia, and Lithuania
to Palestine. The British government would also like to
know how the German government is disposed towards an
evacuation of Jewish children from Germany, Denmark and
the occupied territories of Belgium, Holland, Greece, and
Serbia. Thereupon, says VON THADDEN, the German government answered as follows:

     "Since the government of the Reich cannot tolerate
the fact that such brave and noble people as the Arabs
should be forced out of their homeland by the Jews, those

STAFF EVIDENCE ANALYSIS, Ministries Division.   NG-1704.

negotiations could only be taken up under the assumption
that the British government agrees to send the Jews to
Great Britain instead of Palestine ..." (See notes C & F).

This answer has also been transmitted to the Bulgarian
and Rumanian governments with the request "to either proceed
accordingly or to stop all emigration and wait for the
British reaction". The Bulgarian government has already
answered that it does not intend to deviate from its
present policy of preventing all Jewish emigration.

E – Note by v.THADDEN stating that RIBBENTROP has demanded
that the "FELDSCHER action" (evacuation of 5000 Jewish
children) be submitted to him again, since the British
government has sent another note to "remind RIBBENTROP" of
this matter. The draft of the thesis by Dr.MEGERLE (re
propagandistic exploitation of the British attempt to save
5000 Jewish children) would have to be revised to include
references to the new secret weapons recently employed
by Germany against England. Therefore all records on this
matter will be sent back through Legation Councillor
Kutscher to MEGERLE. Meanwhile the Australian government has requested that the Germans should release 300
Jewish children from France. VON THADDEN suggests that this
matter should be treated in the same manner as the British
request for the release of the 5000.

217

F – Note by WAGNER, states that the Swiss legation has
contacted the German Foreign Office twice in June 1944,
explaining repeatedly that Great Britain is prepared to
accept the Jewish children, and send them to Canada instead of
Palestine. However, says WAGNER, in view of the fact that
there are still negotiations pending with regard to the
permission of Jews to emigrate from Hungary to Palestine,
Group II Inland, (WAGNER) in concurrence with Dr.MEGERLE,
considers the continuation of the FELDSCHER action
(evacuation of the 5000 children) as devoid of any purpose
(unzweckmaessig) and proposes to transmit a further note to
the British by way of the Swiss legation only after the
question of the Hungarian emigration has been settled.
A draft for this note will be submitted to Inland II at
the proper time". EICHMANN, who had been concerned with the
"FELDSCHER action" is to be informed in the corresponding
sense. This note was transmitted by way of the state
secretary (STEENGRACHT) to RIBBENTROP.

G – Note addressed to VON THADDEN states that the propagandistic exploitation of the "FELDSCHER action" should be
delayed until the question of Jewish emigration from Hungary
has been cleared, but "then it should be immediately
resumed".

– END –

Über Herrn Dr.Meg...

Herrn Gesandten v.Sonnl...ther

mit dem Bemerken vorgelegt, daß die Angelegenheit mit
Herrn Colin Ross besprochen werde. Nach Klarstellung
des tatsächlichen Sachverhalts erklärte Herr Colin Ross,
daß ihm die ganzen Umstände der Angelegenheit bei Ab-
fassung seines Briefes an den Herrn RAM nicht bekannt gewesen seien und er nunmehr den Brief selbstverständlich
zurückziehe.

Berlin, den 8. Februar 1944

Thadden

218

1 Anlage

x) ...

z.d.A.

83 -

THF 2140

NG-1794

Herrn VLR Wagner

Hr. Sonnleithner 3/1 ; mit Bezugnahme auf die Anregung des Reichsleiters

Steg 3/5

Empfehle zunächst Rücksprache Chef Sipo mit Wagner. Grundgedanke, dass man nicht nur Kinder, sondern auch Eltern d.h. möglichst viel Erwachsene v. Vernichtungs[illegible] retten [illegible], wohl ist richtig aber fraglich ob diese vorhanden oder [illegible] aus den wirklich Konzentrationslagern ganz nicht beabsichtigt.

[illegible] 3/7.

Inl. II A [illegible] 410 ___ 148

THF 2141

219

Auswärtiges Amt

Nr. Inl. II A 1139 /   den 5. Mai 1944.

220

Bezugnehmend auf die gestrige
Besprechung mit Sturmbannführer
G ü n t h e r wird folgendes mit-
geteilt:

Gesandter F e l d s c h e r als
Leiter der Schutzmachtabteilung der
hiesigen Schweizerischen Gesandtschaft teilte am 2. Mai zu der unter
dem Stichwort "Feldscher-Angelegenheit" behandelten Judenfrage mit,
die Britische Regierung hätte ihren
Standpunkt weiterhin dahin präzisiert,
daß man die 5.000 Judenkinder " in
dem Britischen Reich ausser Palästina
und dem Nahen Orient" aufnehmen wolle.
Die Frage sei nunmehr also für die
Deutsche Regierung die, ob sie die
Judenkinder mit dieser Massgabe ohne
Gegenleistung abzugeben bereit sei.

Die Frage, die die Feldscher-Angelegenheit

1.)   An
das Reichssicherheitshauptamt
z.Hd.v.SS-Obersturmbannführer Eichmann
o.V.i.A.
Kurfürstenstrasse 116

83-84   THE. 3162

Angelegenheit weiter behandelt werden
soll, wird z.Zt. noch im Rahmen des
Auswärtigen Amtes geprüft.

Weitere Mitteilung bleibt vorbehalten.

Im Auftrag
gez.v.Thadden

2.) z.d.A. nach Abgang.

221

THF 2143

Gruppe Inland II

Vortragsnotiz.

Nach Anhörung der in Betracht
kommenden Abteilungen und Gruppen des
Auswärtigen Amtes, schlage ich vor,
Gesandten F e l d s c h e r mitzuteilen, die Präzisierung der englischen Anfrage könne deutscherseits
nicht als positive Antwort auf die
diesseitige Stellungnahme angesehen
werden. Es könne daher nur mit Bedauern festgestellt werden, daß die Besprechungen durch die unbefriedigen-
de Antwort der Engländer als gescheitert anzusehen seien.

222

Weiterhin schlage ich vor, nunmehr die sogenannte Feldscher-Angelegenheit zur propagandistischen Auswertung frei zu geben.

Ich lege gleichzeitig ein von
Kult Pol auf Anregung von Inland II
und unter Mitarbeit von Inf. XIV vor-
bereitetes Manuskript einer Broschüre
zu

- 2 -

zu dem britischen Palästina-Weiss-
buch vor, in welches die Feldschar-
Angelegenheit als Beweis der ein-
wandfreien deutschen Politik in der
Judenfrage gegenüber den Arabern
hineingearbeitet ist. Die Broschüre
soll unter einem schlagkräftigen
Titel - der bisherige "Palästina -
Machtprobe zwischen England und Juda"
ist nur als Arbeitstitel gedacht -
als Veröffentlichung des Institutes
für Geschichte des neuen Deutschlands
oder eines anderen antijüdischen Institutes erscheinen und durch Kult
Pol über die Missionen im Ausland
verbreitet werden.

Hiermit

dem Herrn Reichsaußenminister

mit der Bitte um Genehmigung vorgelegt.

Berlin, den 27.4.1944.

223

444606

Durchdruck als Konzept (R.1.b.)Jo

Ref.:LR.v.Thadden.

bzf. Durchdruck
der Vortragsno-
tiz vom 29.3.
und 27.4.44.

224

Der Leiter der Schutzmachtabteilung der
hiesigen Schweizerischen Gesandtschaft
hat dem Auswärtigen Amt den Wunsch der
Britischen Regierung vorgetragen, deutscherseits möge der Ausreise von 5.000
nichtarischen Personen - zu 85% Kinder
und 15% erwachsene Begleitpersonen - aus
Polen, Litauen und Lettland nach Palästina zugestimmt werden. Weiterhin werde
britischerseits Wert darauf gelegt, die
Auffassung der Reichsregierung hinsichtlich der Abwanderung jüdischer Kinder aus
Deutschland, Dänemark und den besetzten
holländischen, belgischen, griechischen
und serbischen Gebieten kennenzulernen.

Hierauf hat die Reichsregierung im
Januar d.J. wie folgt geantwortet:

Da jedoch die Reichsregierung ihre
Hand nicht dazu bieten kann, daß ein so
edles und tapferes Volk wie die Araber
durch die Juden aus ihrem Heimatland Palästina verdrängt werden, könnten diese
Verhandlungen nur unter der Voraussetzung
aufgenommen werden, daß sich die Britische Regierung damit einverstanden erklärt,
daß

444607

daß die Juden statt nach Palästine nach
Grossbritannien überführt werden und daß
sie ihnen dort die endgültige Niederlassung garantiert."

Diese Antwort wurde auch der Bul-
garischen und Rumänischen Regierung mitgeteilt mit der Bitte, entweder entsprechend
zu verfahren oder jegliche jüdische Auswanderung abzustoppen und zunächst die engli-
sche Reaktion abzuwarten. Die Bulgarische
Regierunghat geantwortet, daß sie von ihrer
bisherigen Praxis, Unterbindung der jüdischen
Auswanderung, nicht abzugehen beabsichtige.
Die Rumänische Regierung hat sich einer Antwort entzogen und praktisch die jüdische
Auswanderung nach Palästine zugelassen.

Am 8. März 1944 teilte Gesandter
F e l d s c h e r dem Auswärtigen Amt mit,
die Britisch. Regierung präzisiere ihren
Vorschlag wie folgt:

" Die Kinder sollen nach England
übernommen werden. Es käme aber für sie
kein Austausch in Frage, weil die Britische
Regierung auf dem Standpunkt stehe, daß
Deutsche nur gegen Angehörige des Britischen Reiches ausgetauscht werden konnten."

Der von Gruppe Inland II ausge-
arbeitete Vorschlag, der abschriftlich beiliegt,

beiliegt, hat nicht die Billigung des
Herrn RAM gefunden. Daraufhin ist ein
weiterer Vorschlag ausgearbeitet worden,
den der Herr Staatssekretär dem Herrn
Reichsaussenminister vorzulegen beabsichtigt. Dieser liegt ohne Anlage im
Durchdruck bei, da es die Anlage bisher
nur in einem Exemplar gibt.

Inzwischen hat die Schweizerische
Gesandtschaft am 6. April schriftlich
und am 15. April mündlich eine abschliessende Stellungnahme des Auswärtigen Amtes
angemahnt.

226

Hiermit

1.)   Herrn Gruppenleiter Inland

weisungsgemäss vorgelegt.

Berlin, den 29. April 1944.
gez.v.Thadden

2.) Wvl....

Ref. LR I.Kl.v.Thadden

Die Engländer haben heute schriftlich die Stellungnahme der Reichsregierung zum Abtransport der 5000 jüdischen Kinder (Feldscher-Angelegenheit) angemahnt. Eine entsprechende Vorlage an den Herrn RAM folgt mit nächstem Kurier.

Hiermit
Herrn Gruppenleiter Inl
mit der Bitte um Kenntnisnahme
vorgelegt.

Berlin, den 16.6.1944.

227

444610

VG-1794

Gr.Inland II   zu Inl.II A 2119.
Ref: LR I.Kl.v.Thadden

Der Herr RAM hatte verfügt, daß ihm die
Feldscher-Angelegenheit erneut vorgelegt werden
sollte unter Beifügung der Vorlage von Herrn Dr.
Wegerle, sobald die Angelegenheit von englischer
Seite erneut aufgegriffen wird. Die Engländer
haben nunmehr mit der abschriftlich beigefügten
Notiz die Angelegenheit in Erinnerung gebracht,
sodaß eine Wiedervorlage beim Herrn RAM erfolgen
müßte.

bfg: Notiz v.13.6.

Der Entwurf von Herrn Dr. Wegerle bedarf nach
diesseitiger Auffassung durch den inzwischen
erfolgten Einsatz geheimer deutscher Waffen gegen
England in Punkt b) unter Umständen einer gewissen
Abänderung, damit er besser in den Gesamtrahmen

228   der vorgesehenen Aktion über die Notwendigkeit
der Vergeltung hineinpaßt.

bfg.gesamten Vorgang

Daher nebst allen Unterlagen zunächst noch
einmal

1) -über Herrn LS Kutscher -

Herrn Dr. W e g e r l e

vorgelegt mit der Bitte, nach Überprüfung
mit Herrn VLR Wagner wegen der erneuten
Vorlage beim Herrn RAM Fühlung zu nehmen.
Im übrigen hat die australische Regierung nun gleichfalls gebeten, 3oo jüdische
Kinder aus Frankreich zur Ausreise nach
Australien freizugeben. Inl.II A hält es
für zweckmäßig, diese Angelegenheit analog
der sogen. Feldscher-Angelegenheit zu behandeln, sobald in dieser eine Entscheidung
ergangen ist. Ein Doppel auch dieser Noti
ist beigefügt.

bfg: Notiz v.13.6.

gez. v. Thadden
Berlin, den 2o.6.1944.   444611

NG-1794

V o r t r a g s n o t i z.

Die Schweizerische Gesandtschaft ist mit
Aufzeichnung vom 13. Juni 1944 und mündlich am
19. Juni 1944 erneut auf die Frage der Erteilung
der Ausreisegenehmigung für 5.000 Juden aus den
besetzten Gebieten im Auftrag der Britischen
Regierung (Feldscher-Aktion) zurückgekommen und
hat dabei erneut zum Ausdruck gebracht, die Britische Regierung sei bereit, die Juden nicht nach
Palästina, sondern nach anderer Teilen des Britischen Reiches, z.Bsp. nach Kanada, zu verbringen.

Im Hinblick auf die z.Zt. noch schwebenden
Besprechungen wegen der Erteilung von Ausreisegenehmigungen an Juden aus Ungarn nach Palästina
hält Gruppe Inl.II im Einvernehmen mit Herrn Dr.
Wagerle eine Weiterverfolgung der Feldscher-Angelegenheit im Augenblick für unzweckmässig und
schlägt vor, den Engländern durch die Schweizer
erst nach Erledigung der Frage der ungarischen
Juden eine weitere Mitteilung zukommen zu lassen.
Ein Entwurf hierzu wird Inl.II zu gegebener Zeit
vorlegen.

Weiterhin wird um Ermächtigung gebeten, den
Reichsführer-SS, der bisher mit der Feldscher-Angelegenheit auf Weisung des Herrn RAM mehrfach
befasst worden war, in vorstehenden Sinne verständigen zu dürfen.

Berlin, den 29. Juli 1944

gez. Wagner

Hiermit

Über Herrn Staatssekretär
zur Vorlage bei

den Herrn Reichsaußenminister

229

444617

LR.I.Kl.v.Thadden

Inl.II A ist der Auffassung, daß propagandistische Auswertung der Feldscher-Angelegenheit nicht angezeigt ist, solange die Frage der Behandlung von Ausreiseanträgen für Juden aus Ungarn nach Palästina nicht geklärt ist. Es ist daher in Aussicht genommen, die Auswertung der Feldscherangelegenheit bis zur Klärung der ungarischen Auswanderung zurückzustellen, sie aber sodann sofort wieder aufzugreifen.

230

Berlin, den 28. Juli 1944

THF 2144

NG - 1794

Zu Inl. II A 2119

Dr. Megerle
BfI Stab RAM

"Westfalen", den 25. Juli 1944.

Notiz für Herrn VLR W a g n e r
=================================

Zu dem Schreiben von Gruppe Inl.II vom 20.v.M. - Inl.II
A 2119 - betreffend Feldscher-Angelegenheit äußere ich mich
wie folgt:

Die für die propagandistische Behandlung der Feldscher-
Angelegenheit gemachten Vorschläge setzen voraus, daß auch
die anderen Anträge auf Genehmigung der Ausreise von Juden
aus dem Reichsgebiet und den besetzten Gebieten sowie die
bei der Ungarischen Regierung gestellten Anträge betreffend
die Ausreise von Juden aus Ungarn im gleichen Sinne entschieden werden. Es geht nicht an, einerseits im AID die Version
zu vertreten, daß der britische Antrag wegen der 5000 Judenkinder mit Rücksicht auf die Palästina-Araber oder wegen
Unzumutbarkeit gegenüber den europäischen Völkern abgelehnt
worden ist, und gleichzeitig anderen Anträgen auf Ausreisegenehmigung für Juden zu entsprechen. Eine endgültige Entscheidung über die Propagandavorschläge in der Feldscher-
Angelegenheit ist daher erst möglich, wenn über den Gesamtkomplex eine Entscheidung getroffen ist. Fällt diese Entscheidung im negativen Sinne aus, d.h. im Sinne einer Ablehnung der Anträge, so ist weiter zu prüfen, ob die Feldscher-
Angelegenheit im AID gesondert zu behandln ist oder ob es nicht
zweckmäßiger ist, die Feldscher-Angelegenheit nicht heraus-
zugreifen, sondern den Gesamtkomplex im Sinne der für die Feldscher-Angelegenheit gemachten Vorschläge im AID zu behandln.

Megerle

THF 2145

231

OFFICE OF CHIEF OF COUNSEL
FOR WAR CRIMES
APO 696-A ·   U.S.ARMY

STAFF EVIDENCE ANALYSIS, Ministries Division.

                                By: Mark Schafer
                                Date: 15 May 1947

Document Number: NG - 1783

Title and/or general nature: Secret telegram by BERGMANN to
                              the German Embassy in Sofia
                              (von KILLINGER) stating that the
                              transport of 5000 Jewish children
                              to Palestine must be prevented.

Form of Document: Original typescript

Stamps and other endorsements: Signature of Bergmann

Date: 13 February 1943

Source: Inl. II Judenausreise nach
                              Palestina 436777
                              now at: FO-SD, Building 32, MDB,
                              Berlin.
                              (OCC DБT 1941)

Doc. 19

232

PERSONS OR ORGANIZATIONS IMPLICATED:
                              BERGMANN
                              von HAHN
                              LUTHER
                              WAGNER (indirectly)
                              von THADDEN
                              WOERMANN

TO BE FILED UNDER THESE REFERENCE HEADINGS:
                              NG - Foreign Office
                              NG - Political and Racial
                                   Persecution
                              NG - Atrocities

SUMMARY:
      Telegram states that the Bulgarian Premier is to be in-
structed that Germany strongly opposes permitting the 5000 Jewish
schildren to get through to Palestine. Germany in the past has
had bad experiences, since the emigrated Jews always conducted
hostile propaganda abroad. Moreover, Germany wishes to retain
the friendship of the Arabs.

      The rejection is to be expressed in a "courteous manner"
in order that Germany cannot be accused of inhumanity by enemy
propagandists.
      Distribution: LUTHER
                     von HAHN (FILE?)
                     Fol IV (FILE?)
                     Fol VIII(FILE?)

                   E N D

Akt.Z. ....

D III 149 g

Berlin, den .... 194...

.... Februar 3

Diplogerma

Consugerma

Nr. S o f i a

Referent:

U.StSLuther
LS von Hahn

Betreff:

Auswanderung von

5.000 jüdischen Kindern

nach Palästina

Nach Abgang:

- im Doppel
- Pol IV
- Pol VIII

z.Ktn.

Freilassen für die Telegramm Kontrolle

Telegramm (Nicht geh. Ch.V.) Offen
/Z. (geh. Ch.V.)

Geh. Verm. für Behördenleiter

Geh. Reichssache

Geheimsache

Ohne besonderen Geheimvermerk

Nicht
Zutreffendes
durch
streichen

233

Auf Telegramm Nr. 176 vom 4.2.43

Bitte dem Ministerpräsidenten schon jetzt mitteilen, dass wir dringendst davon abraten, auf das Angebot der Schweizer Schutzmacht, betreffs Auswanderung von 5.000 jüdischen Kindern nach Palästina einzugehen. Unsere Erfahrungen liessen die Befürchtung begründet erscheinen, dass diese 5.000 Juden unter englischem Einfluss zu 5.000 Propagandisten gegen unsere antisemitischen Massnahmen erzogen würden. Ausserdem würde das geringste Nachgeben in dieser Frage von den Feindmächten als Schwächezeichen ausgelegt und sofort propagandistisch verwertet werden. Auch vertrüge sich eine derartige Massnahme nicht mit unserer Politik gegenüber den arabischen Völkern.

Bitte hierbei zum Ausdruck bringen, dass es von grosser Wichtigkeit sei, die Ablehnung in verbindlicher Form zu äussern

Der

NO - 1783

Der Feindpropaganda seien möglichst wenig
Handhaben für den zu erwartenden Vorwurf un-
humaner Handlungsweise zu geben. Aus diesem
Grunde müsse auch einem offiziellen Angebot
der Schutzmacht zuvorgekommen werden.

~~Luther~~

Bergmann

234

136775

Entwurf! Ko.

V o r t r a g s n o t i z.

Die Irische Gesandtschaft hat mit Aide-Memoire vom
6. Januar 1944 mitgeteilt, verschiedene Organisationen
seien an die Irische Regierung herangetreten mit der Bitte,
200 jüdisch-polnische Familien und gewisse andere jüdische
Familien, die sich in Vittel/Frankreich befänden, in Irland
aufzunehmen. Die Irische Regierung beabsichtige erst Stellung
zu nehmen, wenn sie erfahren habe, ob die Reichsregierung
den Betreffenden die Ausreisegenehmigung erteilen werde,
sofern sich eine Transportmöglichkeit finden lasse. Es sei
ein vorübergehender Aufenthalt in Aussicht genommen.
Auf Rückfrage hat die Irische Gesandtschaft mitgeteilt, daß
es sich bei den weiteren "gewissen Familien" um Juden deutscher,
französischer und holländischer Staatsangehörigkeit handelt.

Diese Irische Anfrage steht im Zusammenhang mit den
Bestrebungen jüdischer Stellen, eine möglichst grosse Anzahl
von Juden aus Europa hinaus-zu-ziehen. Die dem Gesandten
Feldscher auf die britische Anfrage erteilte Antwort lässt
sich nicht ohne weiteres für Irland passend abwandeln.

Inland II schlägt daher vor, der Irischen Gesandtschaft
zunächst mitzuteilen, daß deutscherseits eine Prüfung der
Angelegenheit erst veranlasst werden könne, wenn die Irische
Regierung die Absicht habe, den betreffenden Juden die
Irische Staatsangehörigkeit zu verleihen und ihnen die endgültige Niederlassungsgenehmigung in Irland zu erteilen. Gleichzeitig wäre dem irischen Geschäftsträger mündlich mitzuteilen,
daß nur im Fall der Verleihung der irischen Staatsangehörigkeit
an die Juden unsererseits eine Legitimation zu der gestellten
Anfrage anerkannt werden könne.

Datum....

Doc. 20

235

Dg.Pol.

       Heute mir vom Irischen Geschäftsträger übergeben.
Hiermit
          über Pol.
          bei Inl. II
vorgelegt mit der Bitte, mich zu einer Beantwortung der
Anfrage des Irischen Geschäftsträgers instandzusetzen.
       Berlin, den 2. März 1944.

236

Copie.

2/12

IRISCHE GESANDTSCHAFT

      Die Irische Gesandtschaft beehrt sich, sich auf ihr
Aide-Memoire vom 6. Januar und ihre Verbal-Note vom 27. Januar
bezüglich der Erteilung von Ausreisegenehmigungen für gewisse
jüdische Familien ergebenst zu beziehen und erlaubt sich anzufragen, ob das Auswärtige Amt in der Lage ist einen definitiven
Bescheid zu geben. Die "Aufzeichnung" des Auswärtigen Amtes
trägt die Nummer Inl. II A 145 datiert vom 14. Januar.

                                   [handschriftlich]

237

Staffelde, den 19. Februar 1944

An das Auswärtige Amt.
    B e r l i n .

LÉGATION D'IRLANDE

BERLIN

     Die Irische Gesandtschaft beehrt sich, sich auf
ihr Aide-Memoire vom 6. Januar und ihre Verbal-Note vom
27. Januar bezüglich der Erteilung von Ausreisegenehmigungen für gewisse jüdische Familien ergebenst zu beziehen
und erlaubt sich anzufragen, ob das Auswärtige Amt in der
Lage ist einen definitiven Bescheid zu geben. Die "Aufzeichnung" des Auswärtigen Amtes in dieser Angelegenheit trägt
die Nummer Inl. II A 145. datiert vom 14. Jan.

238

     Staffelde, den 19. Februar 1944

An das Auswärtige Amt.
    B e r l i n .

Ref. :LR.v.Thadden.   e.b.Inland II

239

Am 15.3. suchte mich der irische Ge-
schäftsträger auf in der Angelegenheit
Ausreisegenehmigung für 1.000 jüdische
Familien nach Irland.

Entsprechend der von Herrn Staatssekretär in der Direktorenbesprechung
mir erteilten Weisung wies ich darauf
hin, daß uns nicht ganz klar sei, mit
welcher Legitimation die irische Gesandtschaft die Angelegenheit zur Sprache gebracht hätte. Weiterhin betonte
ich, daß die Frage sehr schwierig sei
und die Überprüfung ihrer Bitte eine
gewisse Zeit erfordere. Im Laufe der
Unterhaltung frug ich den Geschäftsträger, zu welchem Zwecke denn überhaupt
diese Juden nach Irland übernommen werden sollten, ob man sie dort einbür-
gern und zu irischen Staatsangehörigen
machen wolle, oder ob man sie von Irland nach Palästina transportieren wolle,
oder ob sie bis zum Kriegsende Gäste Ir-
lands sein sollten. Diese Frage wäre für
uns insofern interessant, weil eine Entscheidung

Entscheidung über die Ausreisegenehmigung
für einen Juden, der enge persönliche Beziehungen zu irischen Kreisen hat, natürlich ganz anders zu treffen wäre, als wenn
der Betreffende nach Palästina weiter zu
transportieren sei.

Der Geschäftsträger antwortete mir, vermutlich sei die ganze Aktion nur auf hu-
manitäre Gesichtspunkte zurückzuführen, da
seines Wissens die Initiative vom Roten
Kreuz ausgegangen sei. Im übrigen könne er
weder zu der Frage der Legitimation noch
zu den übrigen von mir gesprächsweise ange-
deuteten Problemen Stellung nehmen, er müsse
sich erst selbst nach den Zusammenhängen
erkundigen und würde mich dann wieder aufsuchen.

240

Hiermit

1.)   Pol I

zur Kenntnisnahme vorgelegt.

Berlin, den 16.3.1944.
gez.v.Thadden

2.) Wvl. 1 Monat.

Inland II

Vortragsnotiz.

Mit Aide-Memoire vom 6. Januar 1944 hat
die Irische Gesandtschaft die Frage angeschnitten,
ob 200 jüdische Polnische Familien aus Frankreich
sowie eine gewisse Anzahl anderer jüdischer Familien seitens der Reichsregierung die Ausreise-
genehrigung nach Irland erhalten würden. Am 27.
Januar hat die Irische Gesandtschaft ihre Ausführungen dahin ergänzt, daß es sich bei den weiteren
Familien um solche deutscher, französischer, holländischer und polnischer Staatsangehörigkeit
handele.

Am 26. April teilte der Irische Geschäftsträger mündlich ergänzend mit, daß es nicht beabsichtigt sei, die Juden in Irland einzubürgern,
sondern sie nur für die Dauer des Krieges aus hu-
manitären Gründen in Irland aufzunehmen. Besondere
Beziehungen irischerseits zu den Familien bestünden
nicht. Weiterhin stellte der Irische Geschäftsträger die Frage, ob die Erteilung eines irischen
Einreisesichtvermerks nicht vielleicht schon ge-
nuge, um die betreffenden jüdischen Familien von
einer Evakuierung

241

Hiermit
über Herrn U.St.S. Pol,
Herrn Staatssekretär
zur Vorlage bei
den Herrn Reichsaußenminister

- 2 -

Evakuierung in die Ostgebiete auszunehmen.
Er ließ bei dieser Gelegenheit durchblicken,
daß man irischerseits mit einer negativen Antwort rechne, die Anfrage aber auf anglo-amerikanischen Druck hin gestellt habe.

Gruppe Inl. II schlägt vor:
Dem irischen Geschäftsträger wird in betont
liebenswürdiger Form mitgeteilt, daß der irischen Bitte nicht entsprochen werden könne.
Auch könnten Juden, denen ein irischer Sichtvermerk erteilt oder in Aussicht gestellt
wurde, nicht generell von einer Evakuierung
ausgenommen werden. Wenn jedoch seitens der
irischen Regierung an dieser oder jener jüdischen Familie, die besonders enge Beziehungen zu Irland, etwa verwandtschaftlicher Art,
habe, besonderes Interesse bestehe, sei man
deutscherseits zu einer Prüfung derartiger
Einzelfälle gern bereit.

Berlin, den 28. April 1944

Abschrift.   ~~Aus dem 08.01.1944 eingetragen~~   B"/₅

Irische Gesandtschaft.
—————————————

B e r l i n .
=========

AIDE-MEMOIRE.

Verschiedene Organisationen sind an die
Irische Regierung herangetreten mit der Bitte,
200 jüdische polnische Familien (Flüchtlinge),
die sich in Vittel in Frankreich aufhalten,
aufzunehmen. Die Irische Regierung hat sich
eine Stellungnahme vorbehalten und wünscht erst
zu erfahren, wie sich die Deutsche Regierung dazu stellt, ob sie diesen Familien, falls eine
Transportmöglichkeit besteht, die Ausreise er-
lauben würde. Es ist eventl. ein vorübergehender Aufenthalt in Aussicht genommen.

Es wird weiterhin angefragt, ob gewisse
jüdische Familien, die sich in besetzten Gebieten befinden, eine Ausreisegenehmigung erhalten würden.

Stafelde, den 6. Januar 1944.

(Siegel)

An
das Auswärtige Amt
B e r l i n

243

Am 26.4. 1944 suchte mich der Irische Geschäftsträger auf
und teilte mir folgendes mit:

Die Irische Regierung habe nicht die Absicht, die Juden, die
sie aufzunehmen bereit sei, in Irland einzubürgern. Man beabsichtige
vielmehr, lediglich sie bis zur Beendigung des Krieges in Irland vor-
übergehend unterzubringen. Enge Beziehungen zwischen diesen jüdischen
Familien und Irland beständen nicht. Es handele sich vielmehr aus-
schließlich um ein humanitäres Unternehmen. Der Geschäftsträger ließ
in diesem Zusammenhang durchblicken, daß die Irische Regierung in
der Frage sehr von den Anglo-Amerikanern bedrängt werde. Weiterhin
teilte er mir mit, daß die in Betracht kommenden Familien, soweit
er wisse, in Vitell seien und ihr Abtransport zwecks Evakuierung in
die Ostgebiete bevorstehe.Ob das irische Einreisevisum wohl aus-
reiche, um die Betreffenden von der Evakuierung zu befreien.

Ich teilte dem Irischen Geschäftsträger mit, daß die Angelegenheit unverzüglich geprüft werden würde. Ich könne ihm jetzt jedoch bereits sagen, daß seine Informationen nicht richtig sein könnten. Vitell sei ein Interniertenlager und aus einem solchen fänden
keine Evakuierungen in den Osten statt. Die Insassen eines Inter-
niertenlagers könnten im übrigen auch nicht deutscher oder polnischer
Staatsangehörigkeit sein. Weiterhin könne ich ihm jetzt bereits
sagen, daß lediglich der irische Einreise-Sichtvermerk oder dessen
In-Aussicht-Stellung den zuständigen inneren Stellen kaum ausreichen
würde, um eine Ausnahme von der Evakuierung zuzulassen. Aber auch
insoweit werde er noch eine abschliessende Antwort erhalten.

Berlin, den 27. April 1944

vorgelegt:

Vallen 13/5 Kluer Es wird gebeten, Ihrer Aufzeichnung vom 28.4.
das Aide-Memoire vom 6.Januar 1944 sowie die Stellungnahme des SD zu dieser Frage beizufügen.

Unter Bezugnahme auf die telefonische Unter-
redung möchte ich anheimstellen, den Vorschlag dahin
abzuändern, daß wir zunächst für die Erteilung der Ausreisegenehmigung der 200 jüdischen Familien nach Irland
eine entsprechende Gegenleistung (zum Beispiel deutsche Militärinternierte in Irland) fordern. Wenn uns
die Iren tatsächlich eine Gegenleistung anbieten sollten,
was unwahrscheinlich ist, könnten wir dann noch immer
das Projekt an der Gegenleistung scheitern lassen, falls
wir an einem Austausch kein Interesse haben.

Fuschl, den 5.5.1944

Brenner

245

Durchdruck als Konzept .   *Zu(II A 1490*

Ref. LR.I.Kl.v.Thadden.

246

bzf. Vortragsnotiz
vom 15.5. nebst Ab-
schrift des Aide-
Memoires.

Hiermit

im Original

Herrn VLR. W a g n e r   *AbG 1/5*

vorgelegt, für den Fall, daß der Vortrag
nicht durch B r e n n e r , sondern durch
den Herrn Gruppenleiter Inland II unmit-
telbar erfolgt.

Die Anregung Brenners, Freigabe von
Militärinternierten von den Iren als
Gegenleistung zu fordern, habe ich bereits am Telefon energisch zurückgewie-
sen. Der von Brenner angestrebte Erfolg,
nämlich daß nicht wir die Angelegenheit
scheitern lassen, sondern die Iren im
Hinblick auf unsere Gegenforderung auf
eine Weiterverfolgung verzichten, wird
durch diese Anregung nicht erreicht.
Vielmehr geben wir der Feindseite nur
die Möglichkeit, uns auf das schärfste
anzuprangern, weil wir von den Iren einen
Völkerrechtsbruch verlangen und Juden gegen Soldaten auswechseln wollen. Meines-
Erachtens ist eine sehr freundlich gehaltene

W V. 1 Woche
30/5

9.5

9.1.V

gehaltene, aber klare und eindeutige Ablehnung, gestützt auf mangelnde Legitimation der Iren, da nach ihrer eigenen Angabe ein Interesse des irischen Staates nicht vorliegt, das einzig Richtige.

Eine beschleunigte Entscheidung erscheint geboten, da der irische Geschäftsträger aus nicht recht erkennbaren Gründen sehr auf die Entscheidung dringt und dies gemäss "Braunem Freund" auf Weisung tut.

Berlin, den 15. Mai 1944.

gez.v.Thadden

2.) Wvl..2.Woche

247

Gruppe Inland II

Die Aufzeichnung vom 5.5. 1944 ist Gruppe Inl.II
erst am 13.5.1944 zugegangen.

Abschrift des Aide-Memoire vom 6. Januar 1944
ist anliegend beigefügt.

Das Reichssicherheitshauptamt hat sich, wie stets
bei Behandlung von Anträgen auf Erteilung der Ausreisegenehmigung, entschieden gegen die Erfüllung des
irischen Wunsches ausgesprochen. Ein erheblicher Teil
der in Vittel untergebrachten polnisch-jüdischen Familien, an denen die Iren durch ihre Intervention
Anteil genommen haben, ist in den letzten 10 Tagen
zum Arbeitseinsatz in die Ostgebiete abtransportiert
worden.

Wie bereits bei telefonischer Besprechung der
Angelegenheit am 5.5. mitgeteilt wurde, hält es
Inl.II nicht für ratsam, eine Gegenforderung bei
den Iren zu stellen, weil eine Freilassung Militär-
internierter einen Verstoß gegen das Völkerrecht
darstellen würde und andere geeignete Objekte den
Iren nicht zur Verfügung stehen.

Hiermit

dem Büro R A M

wieder vorgelegt.

Berlin, den 15. Mai 1944

zu Inl. II a 1406

über Dr. Megerle

VLR. Wagner

vorgelegt:

Der Herr RAM konnte sich mit dem Vorschlag von Inland II, den irischen Wunsch auf Ausreise der 200 jüdischen Familien aus Frankreich glatt abzulehnen, nicht ohne weiteres befreunden.

Da diese Aktion zusammenhängt mit der Ausreise der 5000 Judenkinder, schlage ich vor, die beiden Angelegenheiten dem Herrn RAM zusammen vorzutragen.

Fusch., den 15. Mai 1944.

249

Bremer

Gruppenleiter Inland II.

Der Herr RAM hat in der Angelegenheit Anfrage der Irischen Gesandtschaft auf Ausreisegenehmigung
von 200 jüdischen Familien aus Frankreich entschieden, daß vorläufig
keine Antwort erteilt werden soll.
Es könne erst der nächste irische
Schritt abgewartet werden. Über
einen solchen Schritt soll ich aber
dem Herrn RAM umgehend Vortrag halten. Der Herr RAM betonte dabei,
daß natürlich der irische Geschäftsträger auf das freundlichste behandelt werden soll.

250

Hiermit

Herrn LR.I.Kl.v.Thadden

Salzburg, den 27.5.1944.

Büro RAM,
St.S.,
U.St.S.Pol   ab 31
                5/7
m.d.Bitte um Kenntnisnahme.
        - je gesondert -

LR I.Kl. v.Thadden

Der irische Geschäftsträger sprach mich
heute telefonisch von seinem Ausweichquartier
aus erneut auf die Frage der Ausreise-Genehmi-
gung für eine Reihe von jüdischen Familien nach
Irland an und bat mich, ihm mitzuteilen,

1) ob bereits eine Entscheidung wegen der Erteilung der Ausreisegenehmigung erfolgt sei,die
   er nach Ire weitergeben könnte;
2) ob sich die Juden noch in Drancy befänden oder
   wohin sie inzwischen transportiert worden seien.

Auf die 1. Frage bin ich nicht eingegangen.
Hinsichtlich der 2. Frage habe ich ihm mitgeteilt,
daß eine Beantwortung praktisch nicht möglich
wäre, da uns die irische Regierung noch keine
Namensliste der von ihr gewünschten jüdischen
Familien zugänglich gemacht hätte. Infolgedessen
könne uns auch nicht bekannt sein, wo sich die
betr. Familien zurzeit befänden.

Ich darf um Weisung bitten, ob und gegebenen-
falls welche Antwort ich dem irischen Geschäftsträger zu der 1. Frage geben kann. Die Vorgänge
hatte ich im Hinblick auf die gestrige Bemerkung
des irischen Geschäftsträgers dort bereits vorgelegt.

Hiermit
Herrn Gruppenleiter Inland

vorgelegt.

Berlin, den 8. Juni 1944.

251

LR. I.Kl. v. Thadden   M RAM

        Der Irische Geschäftsträger kam mir gegenüber erneut
    auf die Angelegenheit zurück und bat um Mitteilung, ob
    und in welchem Sinne er seine Regierung verständigen könne.

        Hiermit

        Herrn Gruppenleiter Inl.II

    mit Vorgängen wieder vorgelegt.

252
                    Berlin, den 7. Juni 1944

                        v.Thadden

Leiter Inl. II

Jul 5, 4 1982

Herrn LR.I.Kl.v.Thadden.

Der Herr RAM hat entschieden, daß die
Angelegenheit zunächst einmal dilattorisch
behandelt werden soll. Dem irischen Geschäftsträger wäre mitzuteilen, daß er sich noch etwas gedulden müsse, wir hätten die Angelegenheit an die inneren Stellen abgegeben und noch
keinen Bescheid erhalten.

253

Salzburg, den 19.6.1944.

Gr.Inland II   zu Inl.II A 1982.
Ref.: LR I.Kl.v.Thadden

Betr.: Ausreisegenehmigung für jüdische
       Familien nach Irland.

        Der Irische Geschäftsträger kam am 9.6.1944 fernmündlich
erneut auf die Anfang Januar d.J. offenbar auf anglo-amerikanischen
Druck hin angeschnittene Frage der Ausreisegenehmigung für jüdische Familien aus Frankreich usw. nach Irland zurück.

        Der Herr RA hat nach Vortrag durch den Herrn Gruppenleiter
Inl.II entschieden, daß die Angelegenheit zunächst einmal
dilatorisch behandelt werden soll.

1.)   Hiermit
                        Herrn St.S.
                        Herrn U.St.S.-Pol
                   - je besonders-

        mit der Bitte um Kenntnisnahme vorgelegt.
Berlin, den 22.6.1944.

2.)   z. d. A.

254

Gr.Inland II   zu Inl.II A 1982.
Ref.: LR I.Kl.v.Thadden

Betr.: Ausreisegenehmigung für jüdische
       Familien nach Irland.

        Der Irische Geschäftsträger kam am 8.6.1944 fernmündlich
erneut auf die Anfang Januar d.J. offenbar auf anglo-amerikanische
Druck hin angeschnittene Frage der Ausreisegenehmigung für jüdische Familien aus Frankreich usw. nach Irland zurück.
        Der Herr RAM hat nach Vortrag durch den Herrn Gruppenleiter
Inl.II entschieden, daß die Angelegenheit zunächst einmal
dilatorisch behandelt werden soll.

                Hiermit
                    Herrn St. &.S. vorgelegen
                    Herrn U.St.S.-Pol

                    - je besonders -

                mit der Bitte um Kenntnisnahme vorgelegt.
Berlin, den 22.6.1944.

                                                                255

Ausweichquartier: Gestüt Staffelde
(Osthavelland)

IRISCHE GESANDTSCHAFT
BERLIN

2/12

Die Irische Gesandtschaft beehrt sich, auf die
vorhergegangene Korrespondenz (Inl. II A 145) mit dem Auswärtigen Amt und die Besprechungen zwischen ihrem Geschäftsträger und den zuständigen Stellen zurückzukommen, welche
die Gewährung von Ausreisevisen an gewisse jüdische Familien zum Gegenstande hatten, um diesen zu ermöglichen,
nach Irland zu gehen. Die Gesandtschaft beehrt sich, in
dieser Beziehung ergebenst anzufragen, ob die deutsche
Regierung bereit sein würde, 13 Angehörigen der Familie
ROTTENBEBU Ausreisevisen zu gewähren. Die Gesandtschaft
hat erfahren, dass diese Familie früher in Vittel interniert gewesen war und sich jetzt im Lager Drancy, Seine,
Frankreich, befinden dürfte, ferner, dass alle Familien-
mitglieder südamerikanische Pässe haben.

256

Staffelde, Osth., den 21. Juli 1944

An das

Auswärtige Amt,

Berlin W 8

Auswärtiges Amt

Inf.II A 2531

Die hiesige Irische Gesandtschaft stellte die Frage, ob der in Vittel interniert gewesenen und jetzt sich in Drancy aufhaltenden Judenfamilie Rottenbebu, die insgesamt aus 13 Personen bestehe, die Ausreisegenehmigung nach Irland erteilt werden könne. Nach Angaben des hiesigen Irischen Geschäftsträgers besitzt die Familie Rottenbebu angeblich eine südamerikanische Staatsangehörigkeit.

Um der Irischen Gesandtschaft eine Antwort erteilen zu können, wäre das Auswärtige Amt für Mitteilung dankbar, ob es in Vittel oder Drancy eine Familie Rottenbebu gibt oder gegeben hat, und welche Staatsangehörigkeit sie besitzt.

Im Auftrag

gez.v.Thadden

257

1.)

An

das Reichssicherheitshauptamt,
z.Hd. von SS-Obersturmbannführer
E i c h m a n n , o.V.i.A.

Kurfürstenstr.116

2.) Wv. 3 Wochen

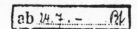
ab 14.7.—

T. 17.8

Auswelchquartier: Gestüt Staffelde
(Osthavelland)

Auswärtiges Amt
Inl. II 2655
eing. - 2. AUG. 1944
___ Anl. 1. Durchschl.

Im Januar d.J. ist die Irische Gesandtschaft vom
Auswärtigen Amt in Dublin dahingehend unterrichtet worden,
dass 200 polnische jüdische Familien in Vittel, Frankreich,
interniert wären. Gleichzeitig erhielt die Gesandtschaft
die Weisung, in Erfahrung zu bringen, ob die deutsche Regierung diesen Familien gestatten würde, nach Irland zu gehen (Note der Gesandtschaft vom 6. Januar).

Die Gesandtschaft wurde vom deutschen Auswärtigen
Amt dahingehend verständigt, dass nur 77 einzelne Juden in
Vittel polnischer Nationalität waren, die inzwischen nach
Osteuropa gebracht worden seien; die anderen Juden in Vittel
seien Bürger anderer einschl. südamerikanischer Staaten,
die zwecks Austausch gegen deutsche Zivilinternierte in
amerikanischen Ländern dort zurückgehalten würden.

Das Auswärtige Amt in Dublin fragt nun an, ob die
in Frage stehenden südamerikanischen Juden nicht dieselben
sein könnten, wie die als polnische jüdische Familien be-
schriebenen, die den Gegenstand der Anfrage vom Januar d.J.
bildeten, und ob sie definitiv in Vittel belassen worden
sind, zum eventuellen Austausch gegen deutsche Internierte
in Ländern, von denen die betreffenden Juden Staatsangehö-
rige geworden sind.

Staffelde/Osth., den 31.Juli 1944

An das

Auswärtige Amt,

B e r l i n W. 8

zu Inl. II A 2655

<u>V e r m e r k .</u>

Am 1.3. erkundigte sich der irische Geschäftsträger bei mir fernmündlich über den
Stand der Frage der Ausreisegenehmigung für
polnische Familien aus Frankreich. Auf meine
Mitteilung, daß Herr LR. v.Thadden sich auf
Urlaub befinde und ich die Vorgänge nicht genau kenne, bat er darum, mich kurz aufsuchen
zu dürfen, um mit mir die Angelegenheit durch-
sprechen zu können. Bei seinem Besuch übergab
er mir die anliegende Note, deren Annahme ich
erst ablehnte. Nachdem Herr Cremin mir jedoch
sagte, daß er in dieser Note lediglich zu
meiner Unterrichtung den bisherigen Stand der
Angelegenheit niedergelegt habe, hatte ich
gegen die Annahme keine Bedenken.

Auf den Inhalt der Note teilte ich Herrn
Cremin mit, daß es sicher das Beste wäre, wenn
er uns eine Liste der infrage stehenden polnisch-jüdischen Familien übergeben würde, damit wir durch die zuständigen Stellen den augen-
blicklichen Aufenthalt dieser Familien können
feststellen lassen. Ich verblieb mit Herrn
Cremin so, daß ich mir die Vorgänge aus dem
Ausweichquartier kommen lassen und ihm dann

einen

259

einen weiteren Bescheid geben würde:

Berlin, den 4. August 1944.

[signature]

IRISCHE GESANDTSCHAFT
BERLIN

2/12

455

     Die Irische Gesandtschaft beehrt sich dem Auswärtigen Amt in der Anlage eine Aufstellung der polnischen jüdischen Familien, die in der Note der Gesandtschaft vom 31. Juli erwähnt worden sind, zu überreichen. Diese Aufstellung enthält die Namen der fraglichen Familien sowie Angaben über die Zahl ihrer Mitglieder und die Pässe, die sich in ihrem Besitz befinden.

                    Staffelde, Osth. den 15. Aug. 1944.

261

An das Auswärtige Amt.

   B E R L I N.

Ref. No.	Familien-Name	Mitglieder	Pass von
1	Berglas	1	Paraguay
2	Beuminger	6	"
3	Blumenkopf	10	"
4	Brettstein	1	"
5	Eck	3	"
6	Eisenzweig	3	"
7	Fränkel	12	"
8	Gehler	3	"
9	Gehorsam	2	"
10	Goldberger	2	"
11	Joskowicz	3	"
12	Kaller	2	" "
13	Kuropatwa	4	"
14	Landau	3	"
15	Lieber	4	"
16	Posnanski	3	"
17	Rapaport	42	"
18	Rozanykwiat	5	"
19	Weinstein	1	"
20	Wolf	5	"
21	Wolman	2	"
22	Frumkin	2	Chile
23	Gorlin	1	"
24	Brinkman	4	Honduras
25	Heyman	6	"
26	Horenstein	2	"
27	Kadycz	4	"
28	Karenelson	2	"

262

138

Ref. No.	Familienname	Mitglieder	Pass von
29	Krystenfreind	5	Honduras
30	Schonberg	5	"
31	Skosowsky	4	"
32	Szeinbaum	7	"
33	Zurawin	2	"
34	Ajzenstadt	3	Peru
35	Dudelsak	7	"
36	Goldstein	4	"
37	Quarlinski	2	"
38	Zemss	3	"
39	Malcowsky	3	Venezuela
40	Brandel	1	Costa Rica
41	Chorr	1	"
42	Fakler	3	"
43	Handelbaum	1	"
44	Lichtman	3	"
45	Nathanson	3	"
46	Rosshandler	2	"
47	Schein	4	"
48	Sohpu	2	"
49	Schwarzbard	3	"
50	Suchestow	2	"
51	Wetsztayn	2	"
52	Zucker	4	"
53	Frucht	1	Nicaragua
54	Kcm	4	"
55	Liscwoder	4	"
56	Fleischer	1	Ecuador

263

Reg. No.	Familienname	Mitglieder	Pass von
57	Neiman	3	Ecuador
58	Tilbor	2	"
59	Wentland	5	"
60	Muszynaki	2	Haiti
61	Naouman	1	Panama
62	Omek	1	Guatemala
63	Schwarzman	1	Uruguay
64	Spinadel	1	Bolivien.
		270	

264

Durchdruck als Konzept (R'schrift.lb.) Ko. Berlin, den 31. August 1944

Auswärtiges Amt

Inl.II A 3114

Die Irische Gesandtschaft bemüht sich seit einiger Zeit um die Erteilung der Ausreisegenehmigung für eine Reihe polnischer Familien, die angeblich im Lager Vittel interniert gewesen sein sollen. Es wurde seinerzeit der Irischen Gesandtschaft geantwortet, daß Vittel ein Lager für internierte Feindstaatsangehörige sei, sodaß polnische Juden sich dort nicht aufhielten. Im übrigen wurde die Frage der mangelnden Legitimation der Irischen Gesandtschaft zur Sprache gebracht.

Nunmehr hat der Irische Geschäftsträger die anliegend beigefügte Liste der angeblich polnischen Juden übergeben, die anscheinend ausnahmslos Pässe südamerikanischer Staaten führen und daher in Vittel sein könnten.

In Anbetracht der besonderen Beziehungen zu Irland würde es das Auswärtige Amt begrüßen, wenn den Iren von hier aus wenigstens mitgeteilt werden könnte, daß sich die fraglichen Familien tatsächlich als Feindstaatsangehörige in Internierung befinden. Sollte eine Nachprüfung keine zu grossen Schwierigkeiten bereiten, wäre ich daher für entsprechende Veranlassung dankbar.

Im Auftrag
gez.v.Thadden

265

1.) An

An

das Reichssicherheitshauptamt

z.Hd. von

Herrn OWR! Kröning

Prinz Albrechtstr. 8

2.) nw. 14 Tage

Im Januar d.J. ist die Irische Gesandtschaft vom
Auswärtigen Amt in Dublin dahingehend unterrichtet worden,
dass 200 polnische jüdische Familien in Vittel, Frankreich,
interniert wären. Gleichzeitig erhielt die Gesandtschaft
die Weisung, in Erfahrung zu bringen, ob die deutsche Regierung diesen Familien gestatten würde, nach Irland zu gehen (Note der Gesandtschaft vom 6. Januar).

Die Gesandtschaft wurde vom deutschen Auswärtigen
Amt dahingehend verständigt, dass nur 77 einzelne Juden in
Vittel polnischer Nationalität waren, die inzwischen nach
Osteuropa gebracht worden seien; die anderen Juden in Vittel
seien Bürger anderer einschl. südamerikanischer Staaten,
die zwecks Austausch gegen deutsche Zivilinternierte in
amerikanischen Ländern dort zurückgehalten würden.

Das Auswärtige Amt in Dublin fragt nun an, ob die
in Frage stehenden südamerikanischen Juden nicht dieselben
sein könnten, wie die als polnische jüdische Familien be-
schriebenen, die den Gegenstand der Anfrage vom Januar d.J.
bildeten, und ob sie definitiv in Vittel belassen worden
sind, zum eventuellen Austausch gegen deutsche Internierte
in Ländern, von denen die betreffenden Juden Staatsangehö-
rige geworden sind.

Staffelde/Osth., den 31.Juli 1944

An das

Auswärtige Amt

D e r l i n   W. 8

Der Chef der Sicherheitspolizei
und des SD

V A 4 b (I)c   4555/44

Bitte in der Antwort vorstehendes Geschäftszeichen u. Datum anzugeben

Berlin SW 11, den   25. Sept. 1944
Prinz-Albrecht-Straße 8

Fernsprecher: Ortsverkehr 120040 · Fernverkehr 126421
Reichsbankgirokonto: 1706 · Postscheckkonto: Berlin 2466

Auswärtiges Amt
Inl. II A 3387
eing. 30. SEP. 1944
___ Anl. ___ Durchs.

An das

Auswärtige Amt
z.Hd. von Herrn Legationsrat von Thadden
o.V.i.A.

in Berlin W8,
Wilhelmstr. 74-76.

Betrifft: Judenfamilie R o t t e n b e b u.

Bezug: Schreiben vom 21.7.1944 - Inl. II A -
- 2531 .-

Die Ermittlungen nach der Familie
R o t t e n b e b u sind ergebnislos verlaufen.

267

.∕.

Es konnten weder in Vittel noch in Drancy
Personen dieses Namens festgestellt werden.

Im Auftrage:

268

LR Dr.Reichel

Der Irische Geschäftsträger war hier und hat
dringlich um Bescheid in der aus der Anlage ersicht-
lichen Angelegenheit gebeten.
Hiermit
Herrn LR v. T h a d d e n
vorgelegt.
Berlin, den 18.September 1944.

(Reichel)

269

Der Reichsführer-SS
Der Reichsminister des Innern

Pol. S IV B 4 b Nr. 2897/44-501-5-.
Bitte in der Antwort vorstehendes Geschäftszeichen u. Datum anzugeben

An

das Auswärtige Amt

in B e r l i n .

Berlin SW 11, den 25.September 194 4 9
Prinz-Albrecht-Straße 8
Fernsprecher: 120040

Auswärtiges Amt
Inl. II *A 3410*
eing. 3 OKT. 1944
____ Anl. ____ Durchschl.

Betrifft: Ausreise ehemals polnischer Juden.
Schreiben vom 31. 8. 1944- Inl. II A 3114 -.

Im Hinblick auf die derzeitige Lage im Westen lassen sich
Feststellungen nach polnischen Juden, die sich angeblich im
Internierungslager Vittel befunden haben, nicht treffen.

Im Auftrage:

270

Th/